Understanding Project Management

Prof Javed Iqbal Saani, PhD

Muhammad Nadeem Khan

ICE

**Intellectual Capital Enterprise
Limited, London**

Published by Intellectual Capital Enterprise Limited

ICE Kemp House, 152-160 City Road

London, EC1 V2N

ISBN: 978-969-9578-04-5 paperback

Printed in England

BRIEF CONTENTS

CONTENTS IN DETAIL

✗

Abu'd-Darda' (RA) said, "I heard the Messenger of Allah, may Allah bless him and grant him peace, say,

1. 'Allah will make the path to the Garden easy for anyone who travels a path in search of knowledge.
2. Angels spread their wings for the seeker of knowledge out of pleasure for what he is doing.
3. Everyone in the heavens and everyone in the earth ask forgiveness for a man of knowledge, even the fish in the water.
4. The superiority of the man of knowledge to the man of worship is like the superiority of the moon to all the planets.
5. The men of knowledge are the heirs of the Prophets.
6. The Prophets bequeath neither dinar nor dirham; they bequeath knowledge. Whoever takes it has taken an ample portion.'"

[Abu Dawud and at-Tirmidhi; Riyadh us Salihin, Hadith 1388, p. 211]

Dedication

To the entire Ummah who has embraced the message of prophet (ﷺ) and is sacrificing because they proclaim that Allah is their Rubb, Quran is their book and Muhammad (ﷺ) is their leader.

Acknowledgement

My gratitude is due to my family who spared me to embark on the project. They also provide valuable information which enriched the contents of this effort. May Allah reward them for their contribution? Ameen! We are thankful to CMP who allow   to us report the case study.

PREFACE TO THE FIRST EDITION

Some factors contribute towards the success of a project. The first is to define the scope of the proposed endeavor in order to delineate it from the other projects. For instance, a chain of superstores intended to open a new store in the downtown. The project needs beginning and ending tasks to determine its boundaries and assign a code to separate from other projects. Secondly, the project is assigned to sponsor to initiate and accomplish the project including delegation of authority to undertake freely various decisions about the venture. Senior managers feel free to concentrate on other matters by making someone responsible. Thirdly, this person applies his knowhow, experience, and insight along with the fundamentals of project management. Finally, organizations launch a project to address a problem (s) or achieve objectives set out for the endeavor.

The book has been arranged around these assumptions. Therefore, addresses the following questions:

What is a project?

Who is a project manager?

What is project management?

Why project management?

What is the strategy to implement the above?

The book offers old principles with different words; however, the arrangement is different from others; the supporting material is recent, and the case study is fresh. The contents are brief where emphasis is on application rather than description. For example, PERT and Gantt chart have been illustrated with examples. Thus, the book is blend of theory and practice; the case study fetches glimpses of practice but theory is underpinning it. The case study itself has been grounded with theoretical support.

The book is a personal guide to us because our micro projects or "to do list" never end and rarely complete on time. We often share with our students that the science is working for people especially the management sciences. Its rule, tools and techniques are applicable at individual, family, and organizational levels. So, learning project management must be applied for us first but it needs clarification of key concepts about the subject than they can be applied at other levels. It coincides with the level of understanding a subject which starts with learning fundamentals, apply them to the discipline and expand it to other situations and ideally in any situation.

We hope the book would serve as a starting point for readers, practitioners and writes. We wish all of them a happy journey to accomplish their projects.

Dr. Javed Iqbal Saani, PhD

Muhammad Nadeem Khan

12 September 2011, Manchester

PREFACE TO THE REVISED EDITION

Project managers are constraints to cost, quality and in time delivery because quality and corresponding cost travel together. Similarly, in-time completion of a project pressurizes both cost and quality. However, this is what they should manage. There is a plethora of literature on the subject, which focuses it from various perspectives. The book is a brief work for busy people. However, it covers essential aspects of the subject. The case study further enhances it; it is a semi-solved case which starts with a problem and suggest a solution. The review questions provide an opportunity for readers to apply what they have learned. It is helpful to understand the subject in a practical way. In addition, case study is a contemporary approach of learning. It virtually takes reader to an organization which is encountering issues and problems and uses various strategies to address them. Thus, managers learn from mistakes and became confident upon successes.

The author has conducted the case study in England which makes the book a unique endeavor on the subject.

I welcome comments and suggestions from academia

and practitioners for further improvements in the future.

Prof Javed Iqbal Saani, PhD
10 February 2018, Manchester

1 INTRODUCTION TO PROJECT MANAGEMENT

INTRODUCTION

Effective management of projects ensues organizational sustainability. Experts evaluate projects on the bases of timeliness, completion at the specified budget and envisioned scope (Rasid et al, 2014). Achieving these parameters need careful planning, execution and monitoring at organization level coupled with project team appointed for the purpose. Prior to that project managers must understand basics to plan and implement projects individually and as a portfolio. This chapter describes fundamentals to lay down the foundations for the rest of the book.

NATURE OF PROJECTS

Juran (1989) views a project as a schedule for solution. A schedule dines the activities and corresponding time of doing that activity, starting, or finishing. This view assumes timing dimension. However, a project is more than that and normally includes many other elements. Andersen (1995) and his colleagues believe a project is a combination of a unique task, is designated to achieve a specific result, requires a variety of resources, and limited in time. Project management institute defines it as temporary endeavor with definitive beginning and ending and creation of a unique product or service (PMI, 2004). A project's uniqueness separates it from routine work and other projects being undertaken in an organization. For example, development of a website for a university is a specific and on-off job of a website developer. A project is also meant to achieve one or more objectives: efficiency, profitability or customer satisfaction. All that need resources: human, financial, plant & machinery, methods, techniques, information and a plan. Finally, it is bounded by time period: a day, a week, a month or a year.   There are various views emerged from it such as:

View I

Project is a problem discovered by senior managers, customers, partners, imposed by competitors, emerged because of government policies, natural

2

disasters etc. It needs a solution and a project is a schedule for that solution.

View II

Project is a unique task, may emerge once in life time of a person which requires resources, bounded by time limit and designated to achieve specific objectives.

View III

Project is a temporary endeavor which has a beginning and ending dates to create a product or render service

Learning (Synthesis)

A project is a unique but temporary problem to be resolved by an individual or organization within given time and appropriate resources.

PROJECT MANAGEMENT

Project management is "the application of knowledge, skills, tools, and techniques to project requirements" (PMI, 2004). Project management is "The planning, organization, monitoring and control of all aspects of a project and the motivation of all involved to achieve the project objectives safely and within agreed time, cost and performance criteria. The project manager is the single point of responsibility for achieving this." (UKBoK, 1995) Andersen and his colleagues (1995) argue that project management involves planning, organizing and controlling. Planning involves deciding in advance what to do, when to do, where to do, who is to do. Planning is the first step; hence, its effectiveness influences subsequent phases and ultimately performance of the project as well as organization. Organizing encompass assigning the responsibilities of a project team to constituent members after building such a team. And controlling involves ensuring that things are done according to plan; and taking corrective actions in case of any discrepancy (See Exhibit 1).

Exhibit 1 Project management

View I

The application of knowledge, skills, tools, and techniques to meet project requirements.

View II

The planning, organizing, monitoring and control of a project and the motivation of all involved to achieve the project objectives safely and within time, cost and performance criteria.

View III

Project management involves planning, organizing and controlling of a project.

Learning (synthesis) project management is the

application of managerial functions and capabilities as well as techniques for the completion of a specific project within agreed upon constraints (cost, budget and time).

Project management is a broad term applicable to the national and international levels; when two or more nations undertake an organized venture with clear objectives, resources, and period, it is an international project. United Nations initiates such projects in developing countries to reduce poverty or enhance welfare of people. Sometimes business organizations undertake a project with international companies; British Aerospace (BAe), developed EU2000 fighter with the help of German, Italian and Spanish partners. There are also some examples of project undertaken by a political or economic block of countries such as OPEC, EU, ASEAN, SAARC etc.; they are multinational projects.

Apart from that, countries initiate national or provisional projects according to their political system of government. Any project undertaken by the federal government is a federal project and any project undertaken by any of the states is a state project (See Exhibit 2).

Exhibit 2 Types of projects	
Region based	National and international
Organization oriented	Single organization and inter-organization
Control	Federal/provisional
Management	Individual/team

Countries initiate projects to improve communication, construction, education, defense capability, social welfare, health, and social responsibility. Their purpose is to increase the facilities of the nation and enhance standard of living of people or quality of life. In business organizations launch projects to increase the wealth of owners (See Exhibit 3). They work as a machine to generate additional resources to inject the fresh blood in the body of the organizational machine to keep it healthy and make the company wealthy. Business organizations launch a project with the assumption that it will be viable, profitable, and manageable. The purpose of feasibility study prior to launching a project is to validate or make sure that the assumptions are achievable within the resource constraints and time involved. Business organizations normally initiate projects for a range of goals (See Exhibit 3 and 4).

Exhibit 3 Project goals

Organizational goals	Nation's goals
Increase wealth of shareholders	Enhance standard of living
Gain competitiveness	Eliminate poverty
Challenge competition	Increase export

Exhibit 4 Organoiron oriented goals

Entering a new market	Installation of a new machines	New software development
Training programme	Implementation of quality programme	Change initiative
Management development	Compliance with new government regulations	New product development

Each of the above projects requires unique combination of resources according to their requirements (See Exhibit 5). For example, quality means consistency of outcomes according to the standard defined. Companies manufacture and deliver products through one or more business processes; each process should implement quality standards to achieve efficiency and ultimately competitiveness in the industry. A company should introduce new projects to support its business network, suppliers, and customer. The success and failure of a vital project creates impacts on the businesses of these organizations.

Exhibit 5 Project resources	
Physical	**Conceptual**
Human	Buy-in of senior managers
Plant and machinery	Customer support
Funding	Support of business partners
	Government approval
	Strategy

It may be worthwhile to remember that country level projects aiming at national development are different from organizational projects due to amount of resources. The outcome of a project in an organization is much more risky than national projects; the nations can cope with failure of a project but an organization may not. There are numerous examples of projects whose failure lead an organization to the jaws of bankruptcy or long-term turmoil. While many nations of the world lost resources on a venture that ended up in humiliation, failure, and loss of enormous amount of human and monetary resources. The United States lost thousands of personnel and billions of dollars in foreign wars; nevertheless, such failure did not threaten the existence of the country or did not put existence at risk. It gives project manager a serious message that they should plan and implement a project very carefully to avoid such consequences.

NEED FOR PROJECT MANAGEMENT

Project management offers tangible and intangible value to organizations; they realize   return on investment, metrics of balance scorecard, and organizational competencies. Intangible gains are lies in change in corporate culture, efficiency, customer satisfaction, learning and growth, competitive advantage (Zhai et al, 2009). Thomas and Mullaly (2007) suggest five levels of value: satisfaction, aligned use of practices, process outcomes, business outcomes and return on investment. It includes both process results and business outcome i.e. tangible financial returns to intangible organizational benefits. Andersen   and Vaagaasar (2009) grouped the contribution of PM into economic, institutional and innovation   perspectives.   Cost/benefit   analysis determine economic benefits. Organizations make investment decision in their best interest which is influence by the size and the importance of projects. The societal expectations and pressure guides the flow of funds in a certain direction, the institutional perspective. The innovation perspective dictates injection of new ideas and technologies as a process of adoption of innovation. Zhai et al (2009) mapped value of project management into four categories: enterprise (improve project performance, competencies of the organization, increased revenue, cultivate personnel, improve customer relationship management, and cultivate favorable culture), customer (realize the value of the project, save project investment, and better collaborative experience), community (avoid conflicts with the community, promote economic and social development, foster talent, improve technical standards, and protect environment), and subcontractors / suppliers (Improve management and technical capabilities and develop long-term strategic but cooperative partnership). Cooke-Davies et al (2009) believes that project is supposed to provide fit between organizational strategy "and the type of project that it executes in implementing its strategy." (p. 110)

Crawford and Helm (2009) identified the value of projects in government endeavors which address accountability and transparency, control and compliance, risk management, consistency in delivery, ensuring value for money and engagement of stakeholders in order to improve good governance.

PROJECT MANAGEMENT IN PERSPECTIVE

Alshawi and Ingirige (2003) describe the historical development of project management that took place successfully across generations. Project management first emerged in the early 1950s on large defense projects and gradually smaller organizations started to adapt the idea. The smaller construction firms operate project management in some form. A great deal of project management involves avoiding problems, tackling new ground, managing a group of people and trying to achieve objectives quickly and efficiently. Let us examine them in more details.

The first era was craft system and human relations that characterized with technological developments to shorten the length of schedule. Job specification developed which became the basis of work breakdown structure later in the project management era.

In the second era, the application of the concepts of management science in the field of project management. Note able developments include introduction of critical path method (CPM) and programme evaluation and review technique (PERT). The purpose of CPM was to identify the most efficient way to complete a project. The DuPont Corporation developed it in 1957 to resolve the problem of chemical plant maintenance.

Why CPM?:

• It provides a graphical view of various activities to grasps a quick view of a project from start to end mostly on a single page.

• It can predict the completion time of a project by satisfying all the requirements at activity level. Each activity assigns the time it needs to complete and its contribution in the entire project. It helps project managers and its team members to conceptualize the project journey with estimated time slots over the life cycle of their project prior to the start of an endeavor.

• It also highlights the critical activities and non-critical activities. The critical activities utilize the actual time associated with them while non-critical activities can be completed during (parallel to the critical activities) the critical activities. The emphasis is placed on critical activities so that the schedule may be maintained. It does not mean non-critical activities are not important or do not need completion; the difference arises in term of total time required to complete a project while the time period of non-critical activities   become part of the critical activities.

The CPM looks like a network of activities and events; the activities are shown as nodes and events are depicted as activities on lines. PERT was also introduced during the period, which is another planning tool for project management.

The third period started from 1980 and ended in around first half of the last decade of the dying century. Invention and affordability of personal computer and associated technologies was notable developments in the period. Low cast multi-tasking and networking facilitated project managers to address complex project scheduling issues. Networking technologies enable various stakeholders to share project information over the desktop; shortening the communication gap and boosting possibilities of delivering the project on time. Project management software was available at affordable prices even to small businesses.

The last period of development commenced with the commercialization of the internet in the mid-nineties; a period of fast interactive and customized new environment, it enables project managers and other related parties to brows, and track projects 24/7 with virtually no cost.

Project management software can be connected with the Internet; it allows automatic uploading of project data so that people can input assigned task, find out the progress of the project, able to know any delays or advances in the schedule, and work for a project in addition to their routine assignments even from their own homes.

In short, this era characterized with productivity, efficiency and client orientation thus focused on project triangle: cost, quality and in time delivery. It opens more dimensions for research and development in project planning, organization, and control. Haughey (2010) has also compiled other developments in project management.

2 ROLE OF PROJECT MANAGER

INTRODUCTION

Projects managers are responsible to initiate, design, complete and terminate projects. They mobilize resources, decide timings of various activities, and provide guidance to people working in the project. It is essential for them to understand their role so that they can manage projects effectively. Purpose of this chapter is to outline key functions and responsibilities of project manager, which is not an exhaustive list but examines some important aspects in the current scenario. It highlights the specific areas upon which he must concentrate in addition to his generic managerial activities.

ROLE OF PROJECT MANAGER

Project manager is responsible to perform basic business functions such as planning, organizing, leading/directing, and controlling in project perspective. *Planning* involves deciding in advance what to do, how to do, who is to do and when to do. It is associated with a task and related time involved. Certain people are assigned specific activities or tasks. They are equipped with necessary resources for accomplishing the job. *Organizing* involves dividing the project into manageable chunks, which are performed by individuals and teams. The job of a project manager is to break the entire project into milestones, tasks or activities and then form one or more teams to manage them. Teams are formed according to the nature of project for products, geographical regions, components of a project and in accordance to the functions or business processes. Each team must be motivated, trained, and coached for their area of responsibility. The project manager coordinates his activities with the team; provides guidance, resources, and psychological support to keep the members of the team motivated and on the track. A project manager also provides *leadership* role to the project team(s); a leader clarifies role to his team members, define or help them to define goals within their roles, boost up their confidence so that they can achieve their goals, and ensures that they receive rewards after achieving goals (Smith, 2007).

To do that, a leader must be energetic, tenacious, assertive, proactive, honest, trustworthy, well organized, intelligent, verbally fluent, self-confident, possess interpersonal skills, and must be commercially astute (ibid, p.118). These qualities differentiate a leader from a manager. A leader is considered employee oriented, takes work from people as a human being and takes care of their individual, family and cultural beliefs. But a task-oriented manager wants to improve productivity and achieve organizational goals in a mechanistic way since he/she perceives subordinates a machines or part of a bigger machine, the company.

Controlling involves measuring performance in line with the success criteria defined in the plan of a project and taking required measures to keep the project as planned. Sometimes corrective measures are not required because the project moves amicably; however, project manager must look at the progress of milestones or other progressive parameters to ensure the project is progressing. Alternatively, a deviation from the planned vision must follow by corrective actions. It may include changes in time scale, timings of milestone or inclusion/exclusion of activities or task. These actions are necessary to ensure that the project is progressing in the right direction over its life cycle in socially and economically acceptable manner. Project manager relays on progress reports provided by management information systems or in case of a large project like opening a new location or branch, project information system designed for the specific project (See Exhibit 1).

Exhibit 1 Functions of project managers in managerial context			
Planning	Organizing	Leading	Controlling
Tasks	Teams	Hiring	Measuring progress
Milestones	Individuals	Training	
Activities	Other resources		Controlling actions

COMPETENCIES OF PROJECT MANGERS

Many writers took a different perspective of project manager; they argue project managers must possess a range of competencies in addition to the traditional function. The concept of *competencies* emerged from organizational competencies. Competences are positively related with project management effectiveness and project success (Hartman and Skulmoski, 1999). They state that project management competencies can be viewed from input-process-out framework; some competencies are needed at input level of a project (See Exhibit 2). High quality input would produce, other things being equal, high quality output. They have taken this idea from educational institutes; for example, Oxford and Cambridge universities recruit high caliber students and polish them to produce world class output i.e. leaders, scholars, writers etc. Other organization also follow the same strategy, NASA injects outstanding graduates in its space and related programmes. British Aerospace hire high flyers and pay them premium salaries to retain them over long term. Japanese management practices promise lifelong employment as a part of developing loyalty and commitment.

Exhibit 2 Competency based model of project management		
Input Competencies (Identifiable competencies)	Process competencies (Project managers)	Output (Project parameters)
Knowledge	Planning	Cost
Skills	Organising	Budget
Traits	Leading	

Motives	Controlling	In time delivery
Self-image		Quality
Social role and behaviour		Client specification

According to Hartman and his colleague (1999) *input competencies* include knowledge, skills, traits, motives, self-image, social role, and behavior. Knowledge refers to the specific expertise about project management, mostly imparted by chartered institutes such as project management institute (PMI). The computer age brought software tools in addition to the PMI certification; Microsoft's Project software is easily accessible and handy to learn as a primary instrument. In addition, there is a plethora of software in the current market. Thus, generic knowledge or certification is the first step towards project management. A related competency is the necessary skill(s) related with the profession; Hartman and Skulmoski (1999) believe it is the ability to determine critical path in the project network. It may encompass other subjective abilities in PM perspective such as estimating time-period of an activity based on previous experience or involvement in similar assignments. Many elements of cost determination also need insight on the part of a project manager; the amount or quantity of other non-human resources also needs subjective estimates. In addition, variations (variances) and deviation under uncertain conditions requires non-quantitative approach. Project managers also function as leader who is to keep team members motivated; the level of motivation may be measured by some quantitative parameters such as absences, unit of output etc. However subjective matters like taking interest in project plans, activities and meetings can be judged by a prudent manager since there are little mechanistic instruments available and applicable in small projects or in small organization due to affordability or other reasons.

Traits are another input variable in the process. A trait according to Boyatzis (1982) as referred by Hartman and Skulmoski (1999) is a "characteristic way in which a person responds to a set of stimuli." For example, when she/he discovers a problem, tries to identify its solution. This type of person is a problem solver, problem solving trait makes him distinct from others.

Motives drive behavior that inspires people towards achievements; motivated manager achieve project and individual objective. Measurable objectives need to be assigned to such manager, most probably in the beginning of a venture and can also be reinforced during the life cycle of a project. However, it is mandatory for senior managers (or project manager for his/her team members) to keep the project teams motivated.

The final input competency is the self-image; it is the perception of a person about himself or herself. How well a certain person is contributing towards the success or completion of a task? Sometimes it is perceived as social role in a society, group, or organization; the more it conforms to the societal norms the more it is appreciated and vice versa. Self-image in this contest creates self-control, a rare commodity in the market of management.

Process competencies have extensively examined in project management literature that is normally concerned with planning, controlling and closing of project. This book takes them elsewhere in more detail.

The final aspect of the model is the output of a project; the well-known outcomes are cost, quality, contents and in time delivery. Completion of a project within acceptable range of these dimensions lead to customers / client satisfaction since the outcome is associated with project success criteria or project objectives outlined in the outset. There are three levels of performance: individual, team (there may be more than one team working in a project, for example, in change initiatives sometimes three teams are involved: design, implementation and continuous improvement), and overall project performance.

A project is an organized set of activities; sometimes performed sequentially but not necessarily. It is a system, that is, "a set of interrelated parts that function as a whole to achieve a common purpose" where each part "would have an impact on other parts and the entire system that can work effectively if the individual parts work effectively and cooperative." (Smith, 2007). However, project manager compromise about high performance of some components against low performance of other components provided the sum is equal to the success criteria. Exhibit 3 summarizes key responsibilities of a project manager.

Exhibit 3   The project manager
View I
A project manager is the one who
Initiate project
Design alternative solutions
Complete a specific unique endeavour
Terminates project
Mobilise organisational resources

Provide guidance

View II

Performers basis business function within project perspectives

View III

Possesses specific competencies

Learning

Project manager is an individual or team who possesses project specific competencies to manage a project

JOB DESCRIPTION

The job descriptions of a project manager have been described under a range of capabilities. They have broadly grouped into four categories: project/practice related competencies (project management, project accounting), career path core competencies (financial management, business development, communication, technical understanding), professional qualities (leadership, teamwork, and client management), organizational responsibilities (innovator development, and internal operations) (www.marisaleseanerou.com, 2010). The totaljobs.com provides a specific list of descriptions (See Exhibit 4).

Exhibit 4 Specific duties of a project manager	
Key Themes	**Details**
Requirement capturing	The client or company's achievement out of a specific project
Resourcing	Deciding the time, cost and resources
Planning	Writing a detailed plan to achieve various stages (milestones of the project concerned)
Team management	Identifying right people for the right job and providing them leadership
Negotiating	Making arrangement for acquisition of material and services
Progress tracking	Ensuring the progress of the project within agreed cost, time and quality standards

Communicating and reporting	Conveying project progress to senior management or clients regularly

Exhibit 5 provides a list of skills and interests needed for a project manager.

Exhibit 5 Skills and interests of project manager	
Category	**Details**
Managerial	Organization, planning and time management
Problem solving	Ability to critical thinking and solving problems creatively
IT Skills	Able to manage project management software in addition to basic IT skills, MS office, the internet e-mail etc.
Focused approach	Able to pay attention to details
Budget control	Understanding and able to control generic and project budget

Technical skills	Relevant to the project, a PMI qualification is advisable
Business sense	Able to understand cons and pros of business world

Besides the basic knowledge and understanding, project manager should obtain either qualification or membership of professional bodies and organizations. Recommended organization includes Association for Project Management (APM), Project Management Institute (PMI), Chartered Management Institute (CMI), and Information System Examination Board (ISEB) for project management in the IT industry. Finally, yet importantly is the practical experience and insight about the job.

3 PROJECT INITIATION

INTRODUCTION

Since a project is a temporary endeavor within a given time, therefore, we can   assume that more than one project may be in progress. Each project has a beginning and ending dates and at least an objective to satisfy its stakeholders (See Exhibit 1) and produce a one-off outcome: software, a building, a road, and repair to a car. They must be distinguishable from one another to manage them effectively; the distinction is made in project planning, organizing, and controlling.

Every project has a different plan, organized in one or more teams, and needs separate measures for controlling. This chapter examines initiation where emphasis is on project selection, project initiation document, and alignment with business strategy.

Exhibit 1 Selected Stakeholder of a project	
Internal	**External**
Managers	Partners
Employees	Public
Entrepreneur	Customer
Internal customer	Government

PROJECT INITIATION

Project initiation is a process of evaluation and selection of projects, which contributes to the overall strategy of the organization. According to the Meredith and Mantel (2010) "project initiation begins with the judicious selection of the organization's project to align them with the organization's overall strategy." Two components are important in the above statement: project selection and aligning with business strategy. Project selection begins with identification of one or more projects, senior management may suggest some project i.e. replacing infrastructure of information technology in an educational institution for modernization and improvement of efficiency.

PROJECT SELECTION

Selecting a project precedes with evaluation: the selection is made on the bases of contribution of a project towards financial or non-financial objectives of the organization. Project selection criteria may be numeric or non-numeric, sometime known as subjective and objective or qualitative and quantitative.

QUALITATIVE APPROACHES

When the rationality is set aside and non-economic reasons because the bases of project evaluation; the subjective guidelines provide the criteria. Meredith and his colleague (2010) put forward an array of subjective methods: senior managers suggest a project which is also known as the sacred cow, project is necessary to continue business (the operating necessity i.e. flood is threatening the company premises, therefore, a defensive wall is essential), remain competitive,(business process redesign was adopted by scores of organization because the rivals were doing it), expansion of the product line (it is usually a part of expansion policy or keeping customer fresh i.e. the company is abreast to competition), and employee welfare benefit projects(establishment of daycare center, a cafeteria, a hospital, a school etc.) They are:

1-Expansion

2-Employee welfare

3-Competitive needs

4-Operating necessity

5-Sacred cow

Management cannot quantify their benefits but such projects are perceived beneficial for one or more of the above reasons.

QUANTITATIVE MODELS

These techniques are on the other end of the continuum; projects are selected on the bases of facts. Some of them are known as accounting method such as payback period(how long the project would take to recover investment; the project with short period are considered favorable), discounted cash flow (what is the net present value of discounted cash flow, the project with positive net present value are acceptable), internal rate of return (IRR) (an alternative discounted cash flow approach; the higher the IRR the more favorable it is and vice versa), profitability index (ratio of cost and benefits; a ratio greater than one is considered acceptable, Exhibit 2).

A variation of quantitative models is based upon numerical scores. The scoring models take into account multiple criteria for selection; they assign numerical values to different components or contributing factor; the project with higher score are selected. Sometimes a checklist is prepared including elements to be considered for selection (most of these factors may be subjective). For instance, to capture potential market share, effect on company image, no increase in energy requirements etc. (Meredith and Mental, 2010). These techniques are both un-weighted factor scoring model and weighted scoring model etc. Exhibit 3 shows a hypothetical case where some selected factors were assigned scores to choose the project. In practice, the factors depend upon the circumstances of the organization or choice of senior managers.

Exhibit 2 Objective evaluation approaches	
A	Net present value (NPV)
B	Internal rate of return (IRR)
C	Payback period (PB)
D	Profitability index (PI)
E	Score-based models (SBMs)

Exhibit 3 Project selection with subjective factors	
Subjective factors	**Score**
Capture market share	2
Customer satisfaction	3
Increasing company image	1
Fulfill social responsibility	2
Energy requirements	4
Comply with Government policy	2
Total	**14**

PROJECT ALIGNMENT WITH BUSINESS STRATEGY

Project alignment implies fitting project to the organization strategy and accommodating the project (a new initiative) in the current operations of the organization. It includes arrangement of financial resources, providing work force, extending support at different level of organization and recognizing its importance at all levels of management (See Exhibit 4).

Exhibit 4 Alignment of business strategies with new projects	
	Adjustment in current business
Current Organizational strategy	Arrangement of financial resources
	Providing workforce
	Management support
	Recognizing project importance

The second significant job of the entire project team is to adjust their project with rest of the organization and to develop project portfolio. Meredith and Mental (2010) offer number of aspects to develop such a portfolio (See Exhibit 5). Some of these factors are related with organizational activities and others are associated with project concerned or pool of other projects. The objective is to find out an optimal combination of projects; some of them offset dysfunctional effects of relatively weak projects, but they are still included in the portfolio for the long-term benefits of the organization or they were "sacred cows", propose by senior managers / owners.

Exhibit 5	Factors for developing project portfolio
Steps	**Related element**
Step 1	Establish a project council
Step 2	Identify project categories and criteria (contribution to organization's objectives)
Step 3	Collect project data (cost data, market benefits)
Step 4	Assess resource availability (both internal and external)
Step 5	Reduce (or rationalize) the project and criteria set
Step 6	Prioritize the projects within categories
Step 7	Select the projects to be funded and held in reserve
Step 8	Implement the process

Project portfolio demonstrates the number of projects in operation and their contribution to the overall objectives of the organization. Exhibit 6 depicts a hypothetical case of project portfolio. Profitability has been taken to reflect the impacts of a project on the overall portfolio. Such comparisons can also be made for other factors to ascertain a combined outcome to make the final decision.

Exhibit 6 A hypothetical project portfolio	
Projects	**Contribution to organizational objectives**
A	5% to profitability
B	6% "
C	4% "
D	5% "
Average	**5%** "

Project A and D are making according to the organizational requirements but C is below it which is compensated with B. All the projects together achieve the organizational average which implies weak project (s) can be accommodated in the portfolio despite an individual project may not meet the criterion of acceptable.

PROJECT INITIATION DOCUMENTS

Project Initiation Document (PID)is useful to define project and its scope, justify the project, a source of securing funding, defines roles and responsibilities of participants, provide information to the people involved to make them effective right from the start of the project (PMI, 2010). Project management institute provides an indicative list of contents of PID for guidance; Exhibit 7 demonstrates them in a summarized version.

Exhibit 7 Contents of project initiation documents (PID)	
Sections	**Details**
Section 1 WHAT?	• Context of the project (background) • Project definition (purpose, objectives, scope, deliverables, constraints, and assumptions
Section 2 WHY?	• Business case (benefits, options, cost and time scale and cost/ benefits analysis) • Risk analysis (risk identification, risk prevention, risk management and risk monitoring)
Section 3 WHO?	Roles and responsibilities (project organization chart/ structure, project sponsor, project manager, project team)

Section 4 How and when	Initial project plan (assignments, schedules, human resources, project control and quality control)

In nutshell, PID "is a guide to a project, clearly laying out the justification for a project, what its objectives will be, and how the project will be organized. This helps ensure that everyone knows what is going on right from the outset." (ibid., p.4) It provides the foundation on which the rest of the project can be laid down.

4 PROJECT PLANNING

INTRODUCTION

Project planning defines the tangible and intangible resources regarding time in various phases of a project. Managers estimate human, material, and auxiliary needs prior to launching a new endeavor in order to provide right amount of resources at right time to ensure smooth progress of activities. It also persuades senior managers to remain committed to support the project and provide necessary financial resources; it is a tool to motivate other stakeholders to continue their support as well. Financiers arrange finance according to the project schedule such as working capital for different activities, milestones and special events. Since borrowing money adds cost, therefore, timing and amount of monetary resources is important to keep the cost slice within acceptable limits. Manager of human resources deputes people for the new project; he hires, trains and inducts additional people to ensure right number of skilled and unskilled employees are available at the right time. In addition, it involves an array of decisions on the part of operation manager, which are largely associated with project plan. Similarly, other participant needs timely information about project requirements so that they can plan their commitments as per plan. In short, the project plan offers guidance to stakeholders to get ready for the new venture in a given time slot over the life cycle of a project.

Caution is required when disruption is possible such as strike by the union, adverse weather, accidents, natural disasters, and regulatory actions (Klastorin and Mitchell, 2013).

PROJECT PLANNING

There are five planning tools for a project which are to be met individually as well as collectively (Johns, 1995). (See Exhibit 1).

Exhibit 1 Project planning tools	
A	Project WBS
B	Project schedule

C	Project objectives
D	Project organization
E	Performance baseline (Budget)

Zwikael et al, suggest another list for project planning,

Project plan, project deliverables, W B S (Work Breakdown Structure) chart, project activities, PERT or Gantt chart, activity duration estimate, activity start and end dates, resources required for each activity, resource cost, time-phased budget, quality management plan, role and responsibility assignments, project staff assignments, communications management plan, risk management plan, and procurement management plan (Zwikael et al, 2005).

Project plans suggest things to be decided in advance "the sequence of activities required to carry out the project from start to completion" (Meredith and Mental, 2010). Plan should contain project schedules, duration, physical/material resources, and human requirements. The plan also needs integration with the strategic plan of the organization and other projects in progress. In addition, Meredith and Mental (2010) believe a project plan should also include summary of the project, objective or scope, general approach, contractual aspects, risk management plan and evaluation methods (See Exhibit 2). This view needs more attention because it encompasses all the elements necessary for planning.

Exhibit 2 The components of project plan
Overall view
Scope and objectives
Material and monetary resources
Project approaches
Contractual aspects
Evaluation methods
Risk management plan
Personnel
Schedule

OVERVIEW OF THE PROJECT

It is a summarized statement of the key facts of the project involved directed to senior management to get buy-in or to continue to support it. It states the goal of the project and develops a relationship with objectives of the organization. For instance, senior managers decided in their strategic targets for the year 2017 that IT infrastructure will be modernized. This will trigger the introduction of the project (Replacement of IT infrastructure); the overview describes it and says that the project is the realization of the strategic target set for the year. The overview describes the milestones and achievements / deliverables associated with them. For example, the project begins with advertising a tender in the press to receive appropriate number of bids followed by negotiation with potential supplier(s) for the purchasing of computers and related items. The negotiation also includes a schedule of delivery, installation, testing etc. The delivery schedule communicates critical steps involved in the project that may be a source of discussion for senior managers; the suppliers earmark the delivery dates; finance department get ready for payment and so on. The delivery-receiving department prepares itself for the expected deliveries and makes necessary arrangement for it.

OBJECTIVES/SCOPES

The project needs demarcation of its boundaries from other projects especially when a joint venture is in operation and many companies are working on a project. British Aerospace (BAe) had a joint venture with four European partners for the development of EU2000 fighter plan. The entire project was divided into four components, each company had to complete one of them, under such circumstances, the part of the project or its component were allocated for each of the partners. Although the objectives of the project were common among the partners but other specific goals were also associated with the individual partners.

Three types of objective are detailed in the scope: profit, competitive aims and technical goals. The profit margin of each organization within their economic and competitive environment is different. For instance, in the BAe case, interest rate was different in various European countries in the recent recession, it affects the expense structure of individual companies in the joint venture. Therefore, the profitability targets were high in the high interest countries and vice versa. The second factor is competitive aim; an organization may be placed under certain categories in terms of competitive position. Kotler (2002) divides companies into four kinds in marketing perspective but they are also applicable to project management: leaders, challengers, followers and niche marketer or specialists in a particular area / segment of market. The leader of the industry would like to maintain its leadership through implementation of a certain project; for instance, a leader would like to replace old PCs with high specification machines or laptops because it might be the contributing factors for gaining competitiveness. On the other hand, a challenger may invest heavily in the technology to get leadership in the industry. There are scores of examples of companies who have invested in research and development (R&D) projects to gain leadership. The most recent example is the Apple Inc. that had launched iPhone, and iPad because of investment in R&D projects. The company had gained substantial market share (21% in second quarter of 2010) because of these projects (Canalys, 2010). Obviously, to continue innovation and improvement of its existing products new projects, will be launched in the future. The third aspect is the specification of technical goals; the famous ISO standards are one dimension of it in addition to the terms of trade between the client (either internal or external) and the project management team. In software development projects, it is known as user requirements, which is the first step for initiation of a project. Upon completion of software projects, the requirements are matched against product features /requirements (Exhibit 3).

Exhibit 3 Objectives of project	
Profit	Leadership of market
Technical goals	Challenging leaders
Competitive aims	Following others

	Specializing in a market segment

MATERIAL AND MONETARY RESOURCES

We assume that a project has been identified, its feasibility was conducted and the senior managers and other stakeholders were agreed to support and provide resources for the project. It may be worthwhile to mention that we are dealing with projects in organization as against projects for national level or public projects, which are normally aimed at improving life style of the people or maintaining it.

For illustrative purpose, let us assume that an educational institute is replacing/upgrading its old IT infrastructure: PCs, server, software, and books. It will be used as an example in the book.

When we think about resources, it refers to the monetary assets: capital expenditures and revenue expenditures. Capital expenditures are incurred on acquisition of tangible assets such as plant and machinery, delivery trucks, computers and software. For example, refer to our computer up-gradation of an education institute, the money spent on purchasing of new computers and putting them in functional condition are capital expenditures. It also includes expenses on transportation, installation and insurance in the transit. In addition, if the said institute chooses to upgrade the existing computers by increasing their central processing unit (CPU), memory, hard disk or any other component than the cost of their acquisition and installation are capital expenditure. The second category of expenditure is revenue expenditure; they are incurred on annual maintenance, wear and tear, electricity, and annual insurance or content insurance.

Project manager estimates both expenditures and document them. He coordinates with the finance department or external financing bodies to ensure availability of funds. Although it is not the authority of project manager to acquire financial resources, yet he must be aware of the process so that any lap in the availability of resources at a time during the life cycle of a project, can be adjusted accordingly.

PROJECT APPROACHES

This part of the plan deals with technical and managerial approaches applicable to the project. The technical approach describes the availability of technology to the project; whether the project is a brand-new endeavor or is an extension of one of the projects. For instance, Microsoft was upgrading its Windows and Office suite; the Windows was mere software which was run by other software e.g. Microsoft DOS (Disk Operating System) until 1995 when the first version of Windows operating system was introduced. It was upgraded with later versions; we have Windows 8 now on the desktop. When Microsoft was extending Windows, the company knew that the technology was available to support their new or enhanced products. For instance, 256MB memory was enough for Windows 95, while Windows Vista required 1000 MB of memory to run it comfortably. Thus, the company assumes that the technology is available when the new version of Windows will be launched in the market.

The managerial approach is related with control i.e. it ensures whether there is a deviation from the routine procedures. Weather the project completes with existing facilities / infrastructure or any subcontractors will be required. e.g. using new supplier for the supply of computers in the case of educational institute but separate contractor will be used for installation / testing.

CONTRACTUAL ASPECTS

It is one of the critical sub-sections of the plan, which includes several documents related with the project i.e. reporting requirements and their detailed description. Meredith and Mental (2010) provide a list of those documents:

1-   List and description of reporting requirements

2-   Customer-supplied resources
3-   Liaison arrangements
4-   Advisory committees
5-   Project review and cancellation procedures
6-   Proprietary requirements
7-   Any specific management agreement i.e. use of subcontractors
8-   Technical deliverables and their specifications
9-   Delivery schedule
10-   Specific procedure for changing any of the above

Technically speaking it is the core of the plan that encompasses not only project elements but also provides the bases for the project organization, and control, the key subsequent phases in project management. For example, advisory committee reinforces the organization structure and reporting requirements laid down for as a foundation for monitoring and control.

PROJECT SCHEDULES

Schedules are the eyes of a manager as the side mirror for a driver; he changes his strategy of driving a project on the bases of schedules; they play a pivotal role in the management of a project at each step of its life cycle. Schedules indicate activities, related resource availability, and any possibility of sharing resources with other projects. For example, the time of IT technician is shared for installation of software on the new machines in the upgrading IT infrastructure case. Since the technicians would perform their routine duties in addition to the replacement project, therefore, their time has to be bought. Milestones and activity schedule are associated with time: beginning and ending dates, and relevant deliverables. Project schedule provides the road map for it.

PERSONNEL

This section deals with human resource requirements; team formation, training, leadership and motivation are famous topics. Meredith and Mental (2010) described following factors as a part of this subsection:

1- Number of people needed
2- Special skills
3-Types of training needed
4- Possible recruitment issues
5- Legal or policy restrictions on workforce composition
6- Special requirements such as security clearances

It is important to match human resource requirements with schedule and budget because they affect cost, which create long-term implications for the project. A time-phased strategy will be helpful to determine how many personnel will be needed and when at various phases of the project or at various milestones. Coordination with human resources department is helpful about these issues.

RISK MANAGEMENT PLAN

Project risk is associated with both potential problems and unexpected benefits on the way to destination. It is a wise approach to anticipate them and make a contingency plan, if possible, to avoid their negative impacts on the project. Meredith and his colleague (2010) identified a series of risks; it includes but not limited to the whole spectrum. They are,

1-   Default of subcontractor(s)
2-   Unexpected technical break-through
3-   Strikes
4-   Natural disasters such as earthquake and hurricanes in a country.
5-   New markets for our technology products
6-   Tight deadlines and budgets
7-   Sudden move by a competitor

Reiss (1992) believes that "a project is a high-risk project if a high proportion of activities have little or no float. "Other believe crises and lucky breaks cannot be predicted, making a list of things "that can go wrong gets everyone in the negative state of mind. I want my people to be positive." (Meredith and Mental, 2010) They also refer Zawikael et al (2007) who found, high-risk project can be managed better through project planning in four areas: schedule overrun, cost overrun, technical performance and customer satisfaction. Better project plans is an effective risk management approach than risk management tools, however.

PROJECT EVALUATION METHODS

Projects are evaluated against their objectives, quality standards and triangular criteria: budget, delivery time and quality. Governmental agencies also demand a given standard to be followed in certain projects; project planners are required to obtain such guidelines and incorporate them in the plan. Evaluation helps to assess a project for monitoring and controlling purpose; it also provides learning for subsequent projects in the organization.

5 PLANNING TECHNIQUES

INTRODUCTION

An effective way to plan and control projects is to use network techniques such as Gantt chart and Programme Evaluation and Review Technique (PERT). They provide a visual deployment of resources, activities and milestones to the project manager and other stakeholders. They are the subject of this chapter.

GANTT CHART

Gantt charts were introduced during first half of the previous century; the exact date con not be determining due to many views of researchers. Some believe it was the work of H L Gantt, other hold an opposite opinion; it was the joint innovation of F W

Taylor (The author of Principles of Scientific Management) and Gantt's work of 1903 or it was based upon the work of Taylor. Irrespective of its inception, the planning technique is known with the name of H L Gantt. It was meant to plan and manage batch production, a production-planning tool. In the contemporary terms, Gantt chart was a time-phased demand dependent planning approach where end-time requirements were linked with constituent components. The purpose was to ensure availability of the components and tracking them subsequently. These were used to plan production on daily basis by determining the quantities to be manufactured. It became the basis of tracking production against goals. (Wilson, 2003). Gantt called it balance sheet as quoted by Wilson (2003), planning and control involves two sets of balances: what an employee was supposed to do and what has been done. And the amount of work to be done and has been done. This was considered the foundation of contemporary Gantt chart. Wilson states "It identifies the items to be produced, the number to be done each day and in total; and the date when production was to start and finish." (ibid., p. 431)

The theory of graphic presentation is useful for comprehensive plan for the entire factory. It implies the job order or sales driven organizations can apply it in addition to project management. Gantt chart is a powerful planning tool for developing project schedules; they are simple and are constructed fairly easy even in complex projects. Each task with its duration is depicted on it. Activities are shown on y-axes and time on the x-axes. The size of the horizontal bar determines the length of time involved in a given activity. The thickness of a bar may show the amount of resources a activity needs or consumes in monetary terms although other parameters can also be depicted. Exhibit 1 shows a simple Gantt chart which assumes that each activity consumes equal amount of resources.

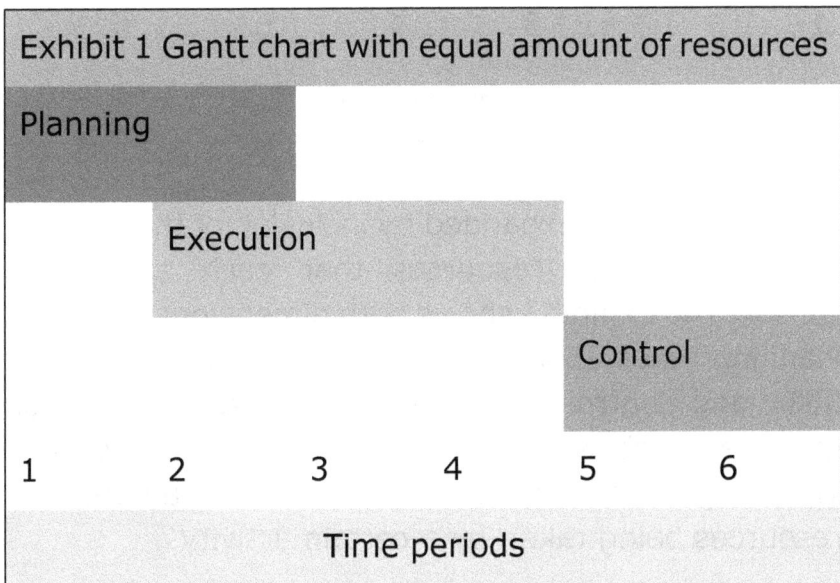

Exhibit 1 Gantt chart with equal amount of resources					
Planning					
	Execution				
				Control	
1	2	3	4	5	6
		Time periods			

The above chart shows a sequential arrangement of three activities in the project where each activity consumes equal amount of resources and the dependencies are simple i.e. execution starts when planning completes. Nevertheless, the activities may be started at the same time and work in parallel to each other (Exhibit 2).

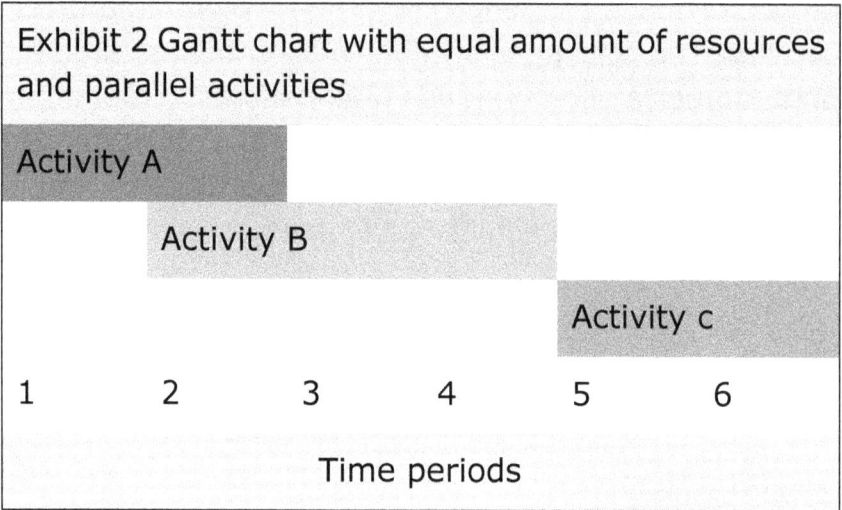

Exhibit 2 Gantt chart with equal amount of resources and parallel activities

Activity A					
	Activity B				
			Activity c		
1	2	3	4	5	6

Time periods

The chart can be expanded by inclusion of the amount or quantities of resources that each activity is consuming. Exhibit 3 shows both dimensions if activity Planning takes 25% of the total resources, Execution 50%, and Control 25%. Execution consumes twice as much resource as planning and control do individually. The height of the bar illustrates the amount of resources being taken by a certain activity.

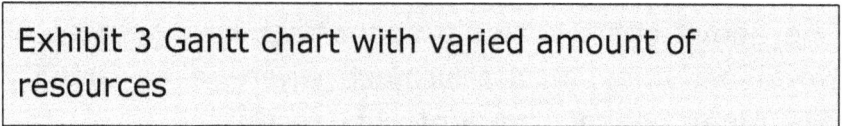

Exhibit 3 Gantt chart with varied amount of resources

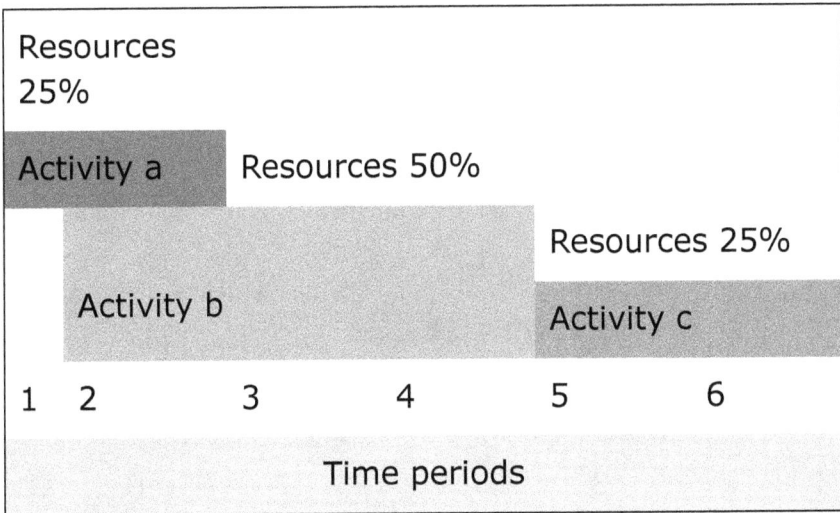

Resources
25%

Activity a   Resources 50%

Resources 25%

Activity b   Activity c

1   2   3   4   5   6

Time periods

Another addition is possible in the chart by dividing the resources into more than one category. Exhibit 4 illustrates three types of resources employed in each milestone.

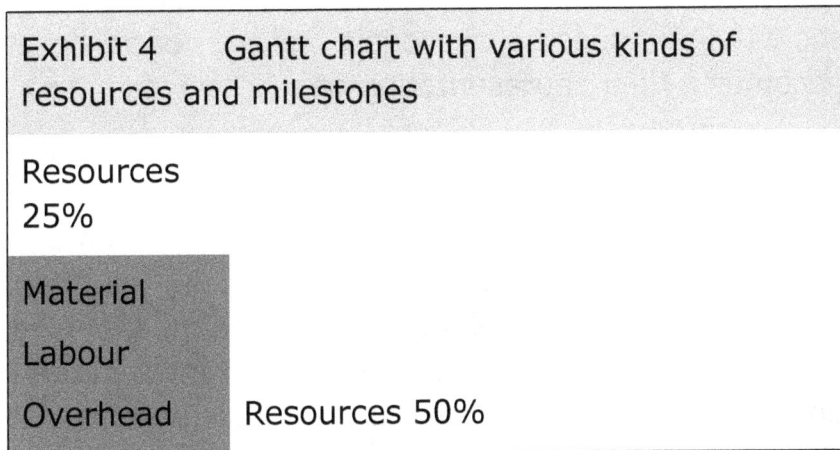

Exhibit 4   Gantt chart with various kinds of resources and milestones

Resources
25%

Material

Labour

Overhead   Resources 50%

(Milestone 1)					
	Material Labour Overhead (Milestone 2)		Resources 25% Material Labour Overhead (Milestone 3)		
1	2	3	4	5	6
		Time periods			

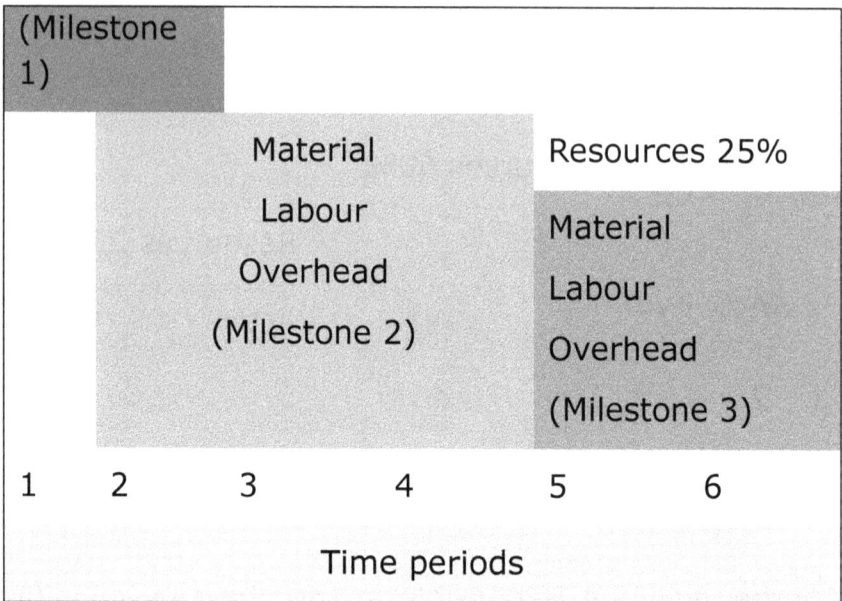

Resources are assigned to each task, which is commonly known as work breakdown structure (WBS). Exhibits 1-4 demonstrate some examples of WBS. In addition, major activities are hierarchically shown into successive levels where each level becomes a finer representation of successive levels.

The "Gantt chart graphically displays the work breakdown, total duration needed to complete the tasks, the resources allocated as well as percentage completion of the project" (Kumar, 2005). The chart is helpful in project planning, developing planning schedules and controlling project costs. Kumar (2005) provides details of how to plan, schedule and control costs in his recent work.

Gantt chart is the most effective tools used in practice (Conforto and Amaral , 2010). Murphy and Ledwhit's (2007) survey of 96 high-tech SMEs in the Republic of Ireland found nine project management tools and techniques: project teams (20), project planning (19), Microsoft project (16), Gantt chart (14), change control processes (10), project control (8), critical path methods (4), stage gate process (4) and earned value management (1). The figures in brackets are the number of companies responded / reported. Fifteen percent of them are using Gantt chart for planning and controlling their projects. Two project-planning techniques were reported: Microsoft Project and Gantt chart. Fifty-three percent of them apply Microsoft Project while 47% use the Gantt chart for project planning. Conforto and Amaral (2010) refer a study conducted by Maylor (2001) which reports that transnational companies use Gantt chart for planning and control of their projects.

PROGRAMME EVALUATION AND REVIEW TECHNIQUES (PERT)

The technique along with critical path method (CPM) is widely used in project planning and control (Omer, 2009). He believes that the most recent project planning and controlling software is based upon the PERT / CMP philosophy. The PERT process consists of eight steps: breaking down the project into activities, determining how activities are related with one another, identifying the sequence in which activities should be carried out, constructing a network of activities and events reflecting their relationships, estimating the time for each activity, identifying critical path (s), re-planning the network by shifting interchangeable resources from non-critical to critical activities in order to minimize the project completion time, and using the network , as developed and finalized to monitor plan implementation during the life of the project (Kuklan, 1993). Exhibit 5 represents a redefined component of these steps (Kuklan, 1993)

Exhibit 5 Represents a redefined component of PERT	
Components	**Steps**
Activities	1-3
Network	4
Estimating time	5
Finding critical path	6
Redefining resources	7
Implementation and control	8

The first three steps are related with activities, the basis of developing a network that is a pictorial reflection of activities with dependencies. For instance, suppose there are ten activities in a project (for illustrated purpose) which can be denoted as a-j. One way to depict them may look like the one which is shown in Exhibit 6. It does not helpful to project manager or other people involved because it reflects activities sequentially. However, it may be meaningful if it is converted to a project network (Exhibit 7).

The diagram depicts the concept of a network. Activities a & f begin together which implies resources are needed for both of them simultaneously. Similarly, b and g can be started upon completion of a and f. Since two activities are starting at the same time, therefore, less time will require to complete the project.

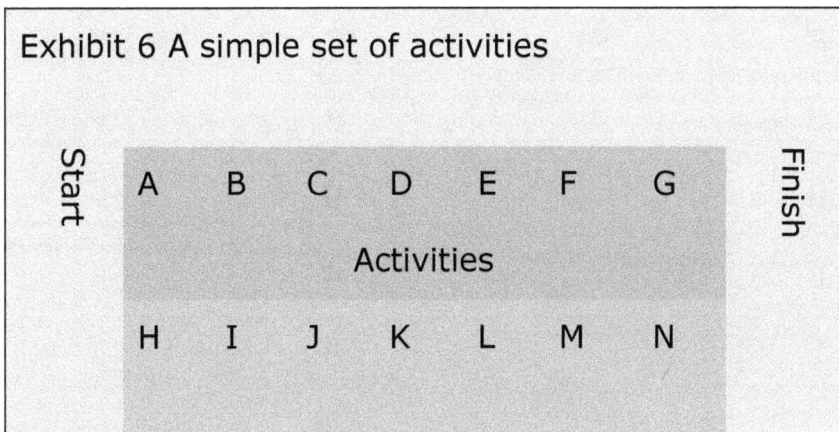

Exhibit 6 A simple set of activities

Start	A	B	C	D	E	F	G	Finish
				Activities				
	H	I	J	K	L	M	N	

The next task is to estimate the timings of each activity (See Exhibit 7). It is helpful to determine the longest path and associated cost of it. During of each activity plays its role in the completion of the project on time.

Exhibit 7 The estimated time of each activity	
Activity	Time (Weeks)
A	3
B	2
C	5
D	3
E	6
F	2
G	3
H	9
I	4
J	3

The projects are much more complex in practice than the one shown here which need more complicated and efficient solutions. Project managers address the issue through network analysis. Exhibit 8 shows a network with duration and the critical path of the project.

Exhibit 8 The network with duration and the critical path

Start	A [3]	D [3]	I [4]		Finish
	B [2]	E [6]		H [9]	J [3]
	C [5]	F [2]	G [3]		

The critical path: C, E, D, I, H and J

More details are shown in Exhibit 9 to understand the CPM and the network.

Exhibit 9 Dependencies of activities

Activity	Following activity
A	E

B	E
C	E
D	I
E	D, F
F	G
G	H
H	J
I	H
J	None

The duration of CP is 30 weeks, the only longest path in the project (See Exhibit 10). It provides a road map to managers for realizing the project.

Exhibit 10 The duration of critical path	
Activities	**Duration**
C+E	5
E+D	6
D+I	3
I+H	4

H+J	9
J+FINISH	3
TOTAL	30 WEEKS

The total duration of the CP is the greatest among the available alternatives. Exhibit 11 demonstrates other possible alternative and their duration.

Four options are available to the decision makers so that an informed decision comes out after the analysis.

The possible parameter for selection of any option is the total score of an option. Thus, option D seems appropriate for the purpose. However, rationality does not work in many situations when constraints overrun the optimal options. It includes budget, union behavior and support and top management buy-in for the projects.

Exhibit 11 Analysis of available alternative

Option A	Option B	Option C	Option D

Activities	Duration (Weeks)	Activities	Duration (Weeks)	Activities	Duration(Weeks)	Activities	Duration(Weeks)
A+E	3	B+E	2	B+E	2	A+E	3
E+F	6	E+F	6	E+D	6	E+D	6
F+G	2	F+G	2	D+I	3	D+I	3
G+H	3	G+H	3	I+H	4	I+H	4
H+J	9	H+J	9	H+J	9	H+J	9
J+FINISH	3	J+FINISH	3	J+FINISH	3	J+FINISH	3
Total	26	Total	25	Total	27	Total	28

Although the critical path is the longest of alternatives, yet it is the most efficient way to complete a project because it saves total project time by 10 weeks while incorporating all activities. Finally, all the activities included in the CP are the critical activities.

The next task is to allocate resources to each of the activities according to their requirements. Allocation is possible based on many factors; some managers allocate resources on the bases of time slot each activity consumes. The rationale for such allocation is that if an activity remains in progress, it uses resources (See Exhibit 12).

Exhibit 12 Analysis of time taken by each activity		
Activity	Time (Weeks)	Percentage time
A	3	7.5
B	2	5.0
C	5	12.5
D	3	7.5
E	6	15.0
F	2	5.0
G	3	7.5
H	9	22.5

I	4	10.0
J	3	7.5

Suppose the total budget for the project is £150m, the amount of budget for each of the activities based on the percentage is shown in Exhibit 13.

Exhibit 13 Allocation of resources based on percentage of time consumed		
Activity	**Percentage time**	**Budget (£Millions)**
A	7.5	11.25
B	5.0	7.5
C	12.5	18.75
D	7.5	11.25
E	15.0	22.50
F	5.0	7.50
G	7.5	11.25
H	22.5	33.75

I	10.0	15.0
J	7.5	11.25
Totals	100	150.0

The network or PERT structures a project, saves time and resources, provides peace of mind to the people involved and materialize the expectations of an organization. The project life cycle is followed in an efficient way and projects are easy to manage.

Project organizing and control is the subject of the next two chapters. There is a famous 'management phrase' that planning looks ahead and control looks back. The next chapter chalks out the bases of looking back.

6 PROJECT ORGANISATION

INTRODUCTION

Smith(2007) defines organizing in a generic perspective, he says "organizing is the process of determining who will perform the tasks needed to achieve organizational objectives, the resources to be used by the way the tasks will be managed and coordinated." There are at least three elements stem from the above statement: determining and assigning tasks, allocation of resources, and deciding management and coordination of both tasks and resources. We will take them in turn in the following lines.

DISTRIBUTION OF PROJECT TASKS AND ACTIVITIES

A project is usually a part of a programme and a project contains activities and tasks. For instance, a university offers many educational programmes, say an MBA; there are many modules in the degree: marketing, finance, IT, management, and others. Each of which is a project for a student. Under semester system, a student should sit in mid and final exams; these can be termed as activities. The same student attends a series of lectures, workshops, seminars, and tutorial, which can be classed as tasks. Sometimes tasks and activities are used interchangeably; Smith's argument supports this view, he implies tasks instead of activities; this book adopts his view and implies tasks (as described in the definition) as activities for the sake of simplicity.

The tasks and activities are allocated on full time or part time basis. Part time arrangements are called integration where "project tasks are executed along with daily work. Project members remain at their desks working in the normal environment." (Anderson et al, 1995). This arrangement is beneficial because the entire organization remains on their disposal of project manager that can be used for the betterment of the project. It also provides flexibility in that the project manager can find suitable people for related tasks, it is easy for him to fit worker to the job and job to the worker. Larger number of people can be involved in the project than a fixed number of team members. The project is considered the responsibility of organization as a whole (See the case study CMP for an empirical exemplar of the strategy), therefore, project members maintain their expertise. Integration creates coordination between project team members and others people (outside the scope of a project). Project members share their problems and progress with other colleague, which increases involvement, a strategy generally used for motivation and boosting productivity. It also enables both organization and project managers to use resources more effectively; many resources such as printers are shared while forming a separate team needs separate printer, for example (See Exhibit 1).

Exhibit 1 Benefits of integration	
A	Flexible
B	Economical
C	Organizational support

D	Shared responsibilities
F	Better coordination
G	Members maintain expertise
H	Better involvement

The other alternative available to project manager is to release project members from their daily work and move them in a project room where they work on the project. Under such arrangements, project team concentrates on a project without external interference and disturbance. However, there are number of concerns about independent project teams. The team does not receive support of others people outside the scope of the project and the project manager may create "state within the state". It becomes easy for him to create a group and gain power, which may last even after the completion of the project. The thinking of project team is restricted within the project and their expertise is no more available to the organization. This way is also notorious for poor utilization of resources especially when some decisions are supposed to be taken by the base organization or senior managers (Exhibit 2).

Exhibit 2 Pros and cons of independent project teams

Pros

Focus on the project

No interference or disturbance

Cons

Less support from outside the scope of the project

Individual influence of project manager

Politics and power play in the project

Team expertise no longer available to base organization

Poor utilization of resources

Slow decision making especially when senior managers are involved in it

However, the choice depends upon the needs and culture of an organization.

PROJECT ORGANIZATION

The next related question prior to assignment of responsibilities is to decide how the project should be organized. Anderson and his colleagues (1995)

suggest two alternatives: hierarchical arrangements and matrix structure. The former is a top down arrangement where junior reports to the immediate senior; it makes a hierarchy or layers of management. They believe that hierarchical structure creates hierarchy or layers of management. They believe that hierarchical structure creates bureaucracy, inefficiency; poor use of resources, outside people in the organization show little commitment for the project and lack of informal contact between the project and its surroundings. Nevertheless, hierarchical structure possesses some benefits as well: describes the responsibilities of various organizational units, establishes chain of command etc. The hierarchical arrangement partly depends upon the nature of organization and its culture.

The second available alternative is matrix organization: it is famous for flexibility. Anderson et al (1995) state that it is helpful for better decision-making, enhanced communication, flexible organization, optimal use of resources, better adjusted to people and problem. According to them, "in matrix organizations groups and individuals are arranged in various constellations of responsibility and authority depending on the matter involved." Matrix structure is useful for multi-product and or geographically dispersed organizations where a product or regional manager heads each product or region. He manages the region as a division where a separate hierarchy exists in the region to concentrate on the geographical area. Similarly, a product manager remains responsible for his product, marketing strategy, customer relationship strategy, promotional strategy and sometimes its financial strategy. However, it misses the merits of hierarchical structure (Exhibit 3). It depicts five elements hindering the true benefits of such a structure; it suggests managers to think about alternative structures for their specific projects.

Exhibit 3 Demerits of hierarchical structure

Bureaucracy	Inefficiency	Under-utilization of resources	Lack of informal contracts	Lack of wider support

Although there are more demerits of matrix organization but its merits out weight them. Which implies it is a suitable alternative for project managers (Exhibit 4).

Exhibit 4 Features of matrix organization

Argument in support

Flexible

Better decision-making

One-to-many communication

Economy of resources

Adjustable to people and problem

Argument against

Unable to claim benefits of hierarchical structure

Although there are more demerits of matrix organization but its merits out weight them. Which implies it is a suitable alternative for project managers.

7 ALLOCATION OF RESOURCES

INTRODUCTION

It is important to allocate resources on the principle of maximization because the performance criteria for a project as well as for a project manager is based upon 'more with less'. This chapter briefly outlines the way that it should happen. The bases of allocation are humans to material and associated time slots.

RESPONSIBILITIES ALLOCATION

The next important job is to allocate responsibilities to various team members. It is assigned through a responsibilities chart, which describes the role of various individuals, and groups or organizations. It explains what is to be accomplished by who i.e. project owner, project director and others. Responsibilities chart consists of details about three areas: principle responsibility chart, project responsibility chart and activity responsibility chart. Principle responsibility chart (PRC) is concerned with organizational, administrative and professional matters and it clarifies the role of various parties involved in the project work. PRC is applicable in departments or managerial functions, resources types (human, monetary etc) and work groups. Project responsibility charts (Pro. RC) highlights the role of various parties for achieving project milestones as defined by the project team. Pro.RC is also developed for functional departments, groups and types of resources. Finally, the activity responsibility chart is concerned with project activities to concentrates on individuals and clarifies their role (Anderson et al 1995).

The purpose of these charts is to organize a large project on the bases of role and responsibilities rather than on the bases of traditional chain of command. The chart(s) pinpoints the part of the job to be accomplished by individuals, groups and or organizations and fixes the responsibilities of the concerned (Exhibit 1).

Exhibit 1 Charts and their purpose

Kinds of charts

Principle responsibility chart

Project responsibility charts

Purpose

Organize a project on the bases of roles and responsibilities

Fixes responsibilities

Responsibility chart contains task reference, task name, and the responsibility of the relevant person. It also indicates the nature of the responsibility: primary or supporting. Exhibit 2 shows a sample responsibility chart.

The chart can be developed for functional departments, cost centers or even divisions (SBU). Similarly, activity charts can be prepared in the same way to assign individual, groups or organization level activities. Responsibility is preceded with authority, which in turn creates accountability.

Exhibit 2　Sample responsibility chart

Task reference	Task name	Person 1	Person 2	Person 3
T1	Gathering information	▭	◯	
T2	Developing model	◯	▭	
T3	Testing model			▭
	▭	= Primary responsibility		
	◯	= Supporting responsibility		

MANAGING RESOURCES

When projects are completed, they become resources of an organization or nation; software is developed for keeping details of employees, students in a college, patients in a hospital. However, prior to completion it consumes lot of resources: caliber of people, plant, machinery, computers, cash, raw material and so on. This section is devoted to a brief discussion of resource allocation.

Reiss states five steps of resource management: defining, allocating, aggregating, leveling, and smoothing (Reiss, 1992). Let us take them in turn.

RESOURCE DEFINITION

Defining resources involves forecasting the probable list of resources. For a construction project, it may include number of engineers, masons, carpenters, laborers, steel fixers, joiners, electricians, painters, supervisors and others. The construction projects consume cement, bricks, wood, windows, doors, steel bars, and electrical material to name a few. Moreover, the most precious resource, the time; how many days, weeks, months or men-hours will be required. Project manager or his team would estimate each of these according to project specification based on their experience; industry parameters or standards are also helpful indicator. Computer software is used at this stage to estimate by hit and trial method. A reasonable list is produced because over estimate increases cost and underestimates increases the possibility of being out of stock. In addition, pessimistic and optimistic scenarios for each of the resources are also developed.

ALLOCATE RESOURCES

The next task is to allocate resources; it implies each task is linked with one or two resources, which have been identified in the previous phase. The resources are allocated on the bases of duration of each activity and work content or workload. Project manager takes each task and allocate resources to them. For example, in CMP case study, cutting whole chicken is a task, the manager assigned four cutters or personnel to it. Since they share other resources such as cutting worktop, knives, cutting machine etc., therefore, they are not specifically allocated to them. Exhibit 3 shows allocation of personnel and other resources to each task defined in CPM case study.

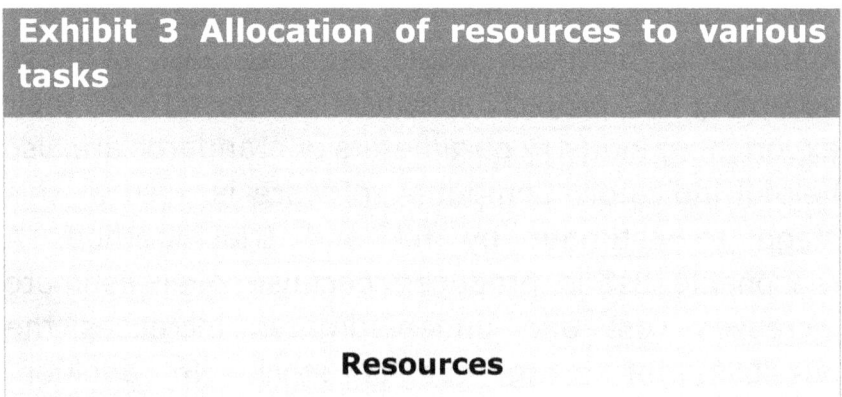

Exhibit 3 Allocation of resources to various tasks
Resources

Tasks	No. Of persons	Worktop	Cutting machine	Cutlery
Whole chicken	4	Shared (all can use it at the same time)	Shared (one can use it at a time)	Shared (used individually)
Boneless breast	2	"	"	"
Drum sticks	2	"	"	"
Mince	2	"	"	"
Chicken wings	2	"	"	"

The duration for all the tasks was equal because the project was to complete within a specified time depending upon the time available to the responsible persons. Sometimes, as Reiss (1995) argues that a particular resource may be needed disproportionately: a particular task may need four personnel in the first week, two in the second week, three in the following and so on. In this case, the project manager should create a resource demand profile that should demonstrate demand of resource over the life of a project.

RESOURCE AGGREGATION

Although total resources are calculated manually for small projects but is a time-consuming job for large projects. The purpose is to arrive at the total amount of resources required for each task on daily or weekly basis. Project management software makes the job easy and provides aggregate resources needed for each task for the desired duration. It helps to compare resource availability and resource demand, a key function of planning and controlling projects and its resources. Project manager can also make "make or buy" decision for certain resources. For example, in construction projects, earth morning machinery is normally hired for daily or hourly basis, contracts may be signed for demand of such machinery with hiring companies so that machine would be available as required on the specified time to make the operations smooth.

RESOURCE LEVELING

Resource leveling is a software function and PC generated report saying the match of resources available and required. Reiss (1995) states that the resource leveling is, "a process by which the software ensures that the project never demands more resources than you have available." Although the software makes things simple by matching available and required resources, yet it delays the project because it takes the task in sequence i.e. the tasks entered in the earlier dates receive resources first. The subsequent tasks are automatically delayed; therefore, some important tasks may be postponed. It requires prioritization of tasks and creation of dependencies to ensure smooth movement of project in the right direction on the part of manager. It is possible manually in small projects but it may create some idle resources. If such resources belong to the organization, as in the case of our case study CMP, then extra resources can be used for day-to-day work. Even if they are idle, they do not increase project cost because they have not specially purchased or hired for the project. However, in small organizations where resources are hired on limited basis; the idle resources increase cost.

RESOURCE SMOOTHING

The final step in resource management is the resource smoothing. According to Reiss (1992), it involves smoothing out "the jagged peaks a trough of the two grams to improve resources utilization ... by adjusting the timing of activities within their float, by moving resources from activity to activity, and by many other techniques such as sub-contracting and prefabrication." Manual alternative may be more efficient than mechanistic solution. Reiss (1992) suggests some strategies to make it more productive: subcontract some resources i.e. hire, take some tasks out of critical path and do them earlier, shift resources from tasks to task and check through your logic i.e. re-examine your assumption about dependencies. In addition, find out alternative ways to execute project, and think how the project plan can be improved in a project team meeting. Process of resource management

1.   Defining
2.   Allocating
3.   Aggregation
4.   Leveling
5.   Smoothing

TEAM IN PROJECTS

A team is a group of people chosen for accomplishing a task, activity and or a project. The team members are selected with the assumption that they are capable, competent and willing to work for a specific job. Previous experience is not necessary for the endeavor but it may be an advantage. The selection is made by immediate head or by a senior manager and the participation can be volunteered to ensure willingness of potential members. Managers apply objective or subjective analysis techniques to check the suitability of potential member. Personal relations, likes / dislikes or other factor leads managers to include a person in his team. For instance, a member may be a "sacred cow" selected and suggested by a senior member of management team. Objective analysis is made because previous experience on similar projects, qualifications, special skills, willingness to join the project and other factors.

A prudent project manager selects right people and keeps them motivated to remain loyal to the project over its life cycle. Project members also need periodic training to get afresh with the changing demands of the job. These elements are examined in the fourth coming paragraphs.

TEAM SELECTION

One of the most important decisions a project manager should make, for the success of a project, is to select the right people. It implies fitting members to the team and team to the member. Two questions are important in this regard: project manager / senior manager or a combination of both select the team members keeping in mind either the subjective or the objective factors. Some employees are volunteered and are free to join a team in large organization. However, it might not be applicable in small organization where a small number of people work and the question of choice may not be possible.

Manager selects team members on the bases of subjective or objective analysis. The subjective approach involves selection of team or any member under four circumstances. People work in organizations in formal ways and informal ways. Informally groups are formed on social, religious, economic, and regional bases. Language also plays a key role in formation of informal groups. When people are associated with any of these perspectives, they want to work with their informal colleagues in the formal team i.e. the project teams. It implies if the selector belongs to an informal group she / he chooses his colleagues from among the group. Senior managers also influenced with such circumstances; therefore, the selectors honor their recommendations.

Apart from personal relations, project manager or senior manager may like the way of working of a person(s) and wants to include him in the team. Again, he picks up the person subjectively. Organizational politics also play some role in the selection since the organization are groups of like mined people who cooperate on matters they like and support the person they happy with. There is no exception for project manager; he needs political support and must include one or more members in his team; in other words, he should inject some political blood in the project team.

Professional manager does not select team members purely on the relationship grounds, they also evaluate them on objective factors.   It begins with collection of data about potential candidates. The parameters for selection range from project management qualification (certification of PMI) to willingness to participate in a project. Previous performance on working on similar projects is considered an additional advantage. Special requirements or skills such as engineers in construction projects and system analysts in software management projects are classic examples. The overall capability is measured by developing an exhibit to obtain a cumulative score that can be a source of selection decision (See Exhibit 4).

Exhibit 4 Skills of a team member	
Objective	**Subjective**
Special skills	Likes/dislikes
Performance	Political reasons
Experience	Sacred crow
Qualifications	Personal relations
Willingness	Affiliation with a social group

Each of the factors needs recognition according to its importance in the selection decision and relevancy for the project. For instance, a score or numerical value is assigned to each of the elements listed in Exhibit 3. It shows the hypothetical values assigned on the scale of 1-5 in a software project, where 1 is the minimum and 5 being the maximum.

Exhibit 5 Allocation of hypothetical scores to a software project		
Factors	**Relevancy**	**Score**
Special skills	Degree in IT	5
Performance	Previous assignments	2
Experience	On the similar projects	3

Qualifications	Membership of professional body	4
Willingness	Agree to work	5
Total		19 (76%)

The candidates with the highest score will be recommended / selected. Bennis and Ward (1997) talked about great groups / teams. They have identified key features of a great team such as ability to work together and the sense of teaming. These features stem from inheritance, training, social circumstances, experience, education and so on. Special needs of a project also affect them.

TEAM MOTIVATION

Motivation keeps the members in the team until the job finishes. People are inspired with monetary, non-monetary incentives and fringe benefits. There are numerous non-monetary benefits offered in employment world. Behavior of manager and immediate supervisor plays a decisive role because employees are knowledgeable and enjoy choice of work. A manager should be a leader who should possess certain features in order to motivate members so that team remains a productive machine for the project. Research shows that people like to be recognized, respected and helped at odd times. Exhibit 6 depicts some of the recent findings about the way employees want to be treated.

Exhibit 6 Features of a team leader for motivating its members	
Area	**Related factors**
Leader related	1.　Recognize individual contribution of members 2.　Each challenge must be a possibility and opportunity 3.　Focus on individual strengths and develop them 4.　Remove obstacles as a super hero 5.　Improve under performers 6.　Work as a part of team rather than its 'boss' 7.　Acknowledge people's contribution regularly 8.　Be the model of accountability 9.　Show progress and communicate it to everyone
Organizational related	Generate clear achievable goals with a reasonable approach

The outcome would come as a collective effort, a spirit every manager wants to inculcate in a great team; great teams believe they are 'on a mission from god'. Well a great idea on its own, deputation from the creator; it implies such teams will be self-controlled because they feel they are accountable to Him. It makes people great, great people form great teams, and the great teams do the great jobs.

8 MONOTORING AND CONTROL

INTRODUCTION

When resources are allocated and responsibilities are assigned the relevant team (s) implement their part of the work. Project manager and others oversee various aspects of paper plan into tangible products with the passage of time. They receive reports about the progress and match them with envisioned or planned version of the project; they take controlling actions (if necessary); this phase is known as monitoring and controlling. This chapter examines key aspects of the phase to ensure that the project is heading towards right direction.

In addition to the above, Meredith and Mental (2010) suggest a cost controlling and monitoring procedures to keeping the things in control. Procedures must be in place to control cost/budget at appropriate levels; milestone is one of the examples to examine reports and take any measure if necessary. Alternatively, periodic method can be adopted as Anderson and his colleagues have suggested a fortnightly review of project activities and taking controlling action as needed. They believe that control must be in place even if no variance is found (Anderson et al, 1995). Greg states controlling project encompass configuration management, change control management, performance reporting, procurement management, requirements management, issue management, risk management and quality management (Greg, 2008).

Monitoring is related with controlling; Reiss (1992) suggests two techniques for meaningful monitoring: do it yourself (DIY) and another people's effort (OPE). The former means to involve the project management team in the process by visiting project site (office, special rooms etc.). For example, for computer procurement project, the project manager pays visit to the officer in charge of purchasing the equipment. The purpose is to investigate what is the progress of the project. Whether the computers are manufactured, are in transit, have arrived and need installation etc. It creates a relationship and enhances communication among team members; become a source of motivation. Satisfactory progress of the project develops a sense of accomplishment and in case the project is not on track, the manager can set new targets.

Efforts of other people suggest examining the progress as perceived or compiled by others, a traditional strategy to monitoring. A better way to address the issue is the combination of both approaches to corroborate what is going on.

The control and monitoring is required to address conflicts in implementation. Common sources of conflict in project implementation are limitation of human resources, different opinions and views, the atmosphere in the organization, unclear responsibilities of participants, 'impose' supplier, classical barriers in communication, administrative procedures, vanity, earlier unresolved conflicts between participants, uninformed, and ignorance (Milunovic and Filipovic, 2013).

PROJECT CONTROL

Project Management Institute (PMI, 2004) defines controlling as,

the controlling processes are those processes that ensure that project objectives are met by monitoring and measuring progress regularly to identify variances from plan so that corrective action can be taken, if necessary.

There are certain key messages in the statement: control is a process (s)of measuring and monitoring progress regularly, the process identifies variances, take corrective action for achieving project objectives. The process starts with monitoring of the progress and translating it into quantitative terms so that magnitude of deviation can be determined. The focus of this effort is to meet objectives of the project in particular and achieving organizational objectives in general. It is an on ongoing process and managers start it from the inception of a project.

The above process sounds good; however, Greg (2008) questions it on the ground that it ignores prevention. He suggests a three-step model to address this issue: prevention, detection and action. He assumes 'prevention is better than cure'; according to him *prevention* is the best way to keep your project on track is to prevent (or at least minimize) variances from occurring. How do you do this? This takes your entire array of project management skills, but a few key activities include investing in planning, communicating effectively, monitoring risk factors continuously, resolving issues aggressively, and delegating work clearly.

Prevention begins with project planning; the previous chapter describes the planning process. Although it seems a pathological solution, nevertheless, it is the only way that leads towards successful completion of a project.

The next step is to *detect* variances; Greg (2008) conceptualizes it as "for this aspect of project control, think "radar system" or "early warning system";

project control should provide early detection of variances. The sooner we can act on a variance, the more likely we are to get the success factor back on track". It needs a mechanism in place, for him,

The key for early detection is to have the tracking systems and work processes in place that allow for the timely measurement of project results. Common examples of detection methods are performance reporting and review meetings. Two important concepts to note here are that to have a variance, you must be comparing actual results to a baseline of some type, and a variance can apply to any of the critical success factors including stakeholders' expectations and quality, not just schedule, cost, and scope.

Once variances are identified, they should be eliminated or minimized to avoid snowball effects on rest of the project.

The third element in the Greg's (2008) triangle is *action*. He believes that it must include, "three most common action ... corrective actions, change control procedures, and lessons learned. Often, as part of the planning for project control, specific variance thresholds are established that dictate what variances and corrective actions can be managed by the project team and what ones need the immediate attention of senior level management." Action is required where variances are identified; Andersen and his colleague (1995) state, the control process must be in place even if no variances are found. Preventive strategy can minimize the probability of occurrence but cannot eliminate the possibility of variances.

Given that let us see an alternative view of project control; control is based upon measurement of progress against plan; if things are not going as intended than measures must be taken to bring them in par with the envisioned parameters. For Anderson et al (1995) control is a managerial activity; it "involves analyzing the situation, deciding what to do ...presuppose that a certain amount of paperwork be done." In case of any discrepancy project or milestone objectives are changed (e.g. delivery time, cost etc.), bringing in more resources to meet the deadlines/ schedule, rearrangement of workload, and changing dates of milestones.

CONTROL FUNDAMENTALS

A reporting mechanism, criteria, documentation required, and communication procedure and tools are key components of control. They are being taken in turn in the following paragraphs.

REPORTING MECHANISM

Andersen et al (1995) believe control cannot work without an effective reporting mechanism in place, establishing control criteria, coordination of plan and reporting. Effective reports apply predetermine templates or patterns for reporting progress. Both good news and bad news should be included in the reports; some project managers believe only good news is not enough, bad news should be included as well to reflect both dimensions of the phenomenon. Reporting not only demonstrate performance but also is a source of motivation and psychological encouragement to entire project team. Formal paper-based or electronic reports and team discussions about performance is highly recommended. It brings out the individual perception of success. Secondly, the experts recommend visible actions to recognize the individual and group input received from teams.

REPORTING CRITERIA

The second element deals with the *criteria* of reporting; project manager decides to review essential matters in advance including cost, quality and schedule. However, other criteria depend upon nature of project concerned. Sometimes the choice of manager plays a decisive role in the definition and selection of "critical success factors" at different stages or milestones.

DOCUMENTATION

Another key principle is reporting on the plans; according to Anderson et al (1995) "reporting should occur on a document which also shows the actual plan. Each time a report is made, it must subsequently be compared with the plan." It ensures keeping the report to the point. Sufficient room should be provided on the plan for this purpose and multiple copies must be made to support the idea. It is important to send deviation / variance reports to those who have authority to take corrective actions or enable to take some step to do so.

COMMUNICATING REPORTS

Finally, reports must be sent at a fixed *interval*; a monthly reporting is appropriate at milestone level while a fortnightly reporting is usually suitable at activity level. Some manager prefers to report when a milestone is achieved. Rozenes et al (2004) found characteristics of a strong control mechanism in construction projects: ongoing managerial efforts to achieving project objectives, allocation of appropriate amount of financial resources, work break down structure must be established hierarchically, project team should be monitored at the work package level. Most important element is the ongoing managerial behavior; some managers believe that control is a periodical job. Examining reports at fixed intervals or milestones is the most effective way; if something goes wrong than corrective measures should be taken immediately. The approach has been criticized on the ground that it multiplies a small problem into an issue that may need significant resources and may affect other activities and milestones. Nevertheless, some managers believe a continuous control system is much more effective than the periodic one where corrective actions are taken without waiting for a specific periodic report (Exhibit 1).

Each column shows a single element related with the procedure.

Exhibit 1 Control procedures			
Mechanism	Criteria	Documentation	Communication
• Good news • Bad news	• Cost • Quality • Schedule	Reporting on plan	• Milestones • Activity • Periodical

CONTROL TECHNIQUES

Tradition methods of project control is associated with historical data, which predict the possible variations in future. They do not consider unforeseen events or "situation they are surprising or develop outside the scope of project plan" (Nikander and Eloranta, 2001). They also argue that these methods ignore human and cultural issues. It is taken in more detail in the following paragraphs.

The control techniques are taken in turn to understand the phenomenon for applying in pragmatic situations in real projects.

A-COST-BASED

Cost-based reporting or simply cost reporting is well known and common in practice. Under the system, the actual cost is matched with planned figures and a variance is calculated. Any positive discrepancy is highlighted and cost control measures are taken if it overruns the planned figures. It also forecasts the total cost of the project due to changes in the cost structure or trend to date. Nikander and Eloranta (2001) questioned it on1` the ground that it focuses on only cost-related matters.

B-PROJECT SCOPE MANAGEMENT

Rozenes et al (2004) describe some more techniques: project scope management (PCM) addresses specific issues to achieve "other" project aims. The PCM defines procedures to alter project content to motivate stakeholders, increase knowledge base, accommodates technological developments, and changes in project process. Another tool is called design review (DR) which involves "a series of design reviews (DR) which typically contains predefined control points through a project life cycle." (ibid., p.110).

C-EXTERNAL PARAMETERS

There are some external control parameters, which are the responsibility of base organization since they are the part of supply chain management and, therefore, considered out of jurisdiction of an individual project manager. The base organization deals with them on an ongoing base rather than for a particular project through five Rs: right quantity, right quality, the right price, the right supplier and the right time and place. (Andersen et al, 1995)

D-MISCELLANEOUS

There are other methods available for examining project performance: bar chart schedule, schedule performance, work performance, the earned value methods and cost/schedule control system criteria. They focus is on project events, an objective analysis of event (s). Nikander and Eloranda (2001) argue that these techniques are useful if used with critical path method.

Saladis (2003) argues the importance of control, he states, "controls should be established for all projects regardless of size. Without control, projects can become wild very quickly and in many cases, trying to regain control becomes an enormous and costly effort." He suggests a series of actions for it.

1-Establishment of control processes (Establish mutually agreed upon monitoring and control processes at the start of the project, develop and communicate a change control process, clearly define an escalation process, and follow it, and separate personal interests from business issues.

2-Team functions   Create a change control team and assign a change control manager, use the expertise of the team for plan development and to identify solutions to problems.

*3-Communication*Communicate the importance of "Freeze Dates" and the consequences of failing to observe them, communication with the sponsor or project executive helps keep things under control

4-Create ownership   Ensure that all issues and action items have owners.

5-Expect realistically   Set expectations early. Set them intentionally, revisit expectations on a regular basis to ensure they are still valid. Reset when necessary

6-Steadfastness Do not keep changing your mind. You can quickly de-position yourself and lose credibility.

9 SUCCESS FACTORS

INTRODUCTION

Although the idea of CSFs was originally coined for management of an organization, yet it is equally applicable to project management. Critical factors play key role in the success of a project, missing any of these may lead to failure or not achieving envisioned objectives. Rozenes et al (2004) report some of them: clarity of goals, management support, ownership, a control mechanism and communication. Soderlund (2004) adds clear project plans and client relationship; however, "the traditional triple constraint criteria seam to prevail." (ibid., p. 189).

CRITICAL SUCCESS FACTORS

Greg (2005) provides a detailed list of such factors, exhibit 1 classify them in a new form.

Exhibit 1 Critical success factors for a project	
Category	**Relevant factor**
Organizational	• Project is aligned with organizational goals • Project has effective management support. • Proper investment must be made in planning
Stakeholder oriented	• All key stakeholders are in agreement on the purpose, goals, and objectives of the project • All key stakeholders share a common vision on the project results. • All key stakeholders share REALISTIC expectations for the project results. • Each stakeholder and team member's role(s) and responsibilities are clearly communicated and understood

Technical	• The project results meet the expectations of the key stakeholders.
	• Stakeholder expectations are constantly managed and validated throughout the project
	• The project scope, approach, and deliverables are clearly defined and agreed upon during planning
	• Each stakeholder and team member's role(s) and responsibilities are clearly communicated and understood
	• A high priority is placed on accurate and complete work effort estimates
	• A realistic schedule is developed and agreed upon
	• The project team has a strong results-focus and customer-orientation.
	• Project communications are consistent, effective, and focused on "understanding"
	• Project progress is measured consistently from the current baseline

	• Project issues and subsequent action items are aggressively pursued
	• There is a strong sense of collaboration and teamwork.
	• Expectations and changes surrounding scope, quality, schedule, and cost are closely managed
	• Human resources are skilled and available when needed.
	• Project team proactively identifies risk and determines mitigation strategies to reduce project exposure.
	• Project team anticipates and overcomes obstacles to ensure project meets objectives.
Managerial	Project should have effective leadership.

The organizational elements are those for which the entire organization is responsible. For example, investment in planning processes, which is the done at strategic level. Since more than one project may be in progress at any given time, the alignment of each of them with organizational objectives is essential to acknowledge the existence of each of the projects. It also motivates the project team in that they are being honored for their contribution. Finally, support of senior managers is a key factor in any of the planned change initiative and project management has no exception.

Furthermore, Greg (2005) summarizes characteristics of a successful project: all the deliverables are delivered as stated, it is completed as per schedule, the project does not overrun the envisioned budget, the project meets all the functional and quality specifications, achieves its objectives, goals and purposes, meets expectations of key stakeholders and clients, and maintains win-win relationship. He says win-win relationships implies "the needs of the project are met with a "people focus" and do not require sacrificing the needs of individual team members or vendors. Participants on successful projects should be enthusiastic when the project is complete and eager to repeat a similar experience. "It suggests that the project team and key stakeholders including clients should define and agree success criteria prior to commencement of a project.

REASONS FOR PROJECTS FAILURE

Projects failure rate varies from 28.5% to 57.3% due to numerous reasons in software field as reported by Ambler (2008). Hameri (1997) states some of them:

ignorance of what other project teams are doing; lack of discipline in design change control; diverse views on what are the objectives of the project; rigid project planning and scheduling routines; poor reactivity to sudden changes in the project environment; and unforeseen technological difficulties.

The generic criterion for unsuccessful project is not meeting triple constraints: not completing on time with budget and not meeting quality standards. In addition, Azzopardi (2010) reports a detailed account of reasons for failure of projects:

(a) Lack of a valid business case justifying the project

(b) Objectives not properly defined and agreed

(c) Lack of communication and stakeholder management

(d) Outcomes and/or benefits not properly defined in measurable terms

(e) Lack of quality control

(f) Poor estimation of duration and cost

(g) Inadequate definition and acceptance of roles (governance)

(h) Insufficient planning and coordination of resources

Most of these are causes occur at the planning stage except c and e. For example, if objectives (achievements) are not defined and agreed with stakeholders, the project team cannot visualize what to achieve. Everyone will be working in his/her own direction or employees would define their own objectives. Project objective provide target (s) which define tasks and activities; wrong objectives lead to wrong tasks and activities. It leads to waste of time and efforts in both defining and performing activities and tasks. In other words, absence of right objectives could lead to failure. So, it is necessary to define the objectives in the beginning and make a revision when require.

10 CASE STUDY

INTRODUCTION TO CASE STUDIES

Case study is a business story that describes the stages of a project over its life cycle. Case-based analysis begun in law and medical science. The decision made by jurists became an exemplar for the other lawyers and judges to form their opinion about a certain case. The medical professionals also adopt the same for treatment of patients. It is a recent phenomenon in management sciences; project management has no exception. Case study is also a research approach based on qualitative paradigm. It is widely used for teaching purpose in business schools these days. It is because a business situation is described in a teaching case with plethora of data. The job of learners is to analyze it to gain understanding and identify alternatives in order to arrive a given solution.

Case study is bombarded with data. It may include history of the organization, its products and services, organization structure, customer base, financial management tools, revenue stream; its relations with partners, competitors and other parties in the country or market. Problems encountered and solutions adopted to resolve the issues.

The analysis strategy is generic rather than a specific. Our case studies are partially solved. Here a problem or opportunity arises as a result of an order placed by a customer. The organization forms a team to fulfil it. The team undergoes the project management process. Project initiation, planning, resources allocation and implementation/monitoring and control. One of the case also discusses the risk associated with the project.

The team has adopted one of the many ways available to resolve the issue. Teachers and learners can identify other alternatives to find out other viable solutions. The purpose of the case is not to find out an optimum solution but to follow a process of encountering problems and the strategy to address it. It provides a learning opportunity to apply it in similar situations.

CASE OF CHEETHAM MEAT & POULTRY (CPM)

INTRODUCTION

The principles of PM are applicable in any organization irrespective of its size, nature of business or mode of organization (sole proprietor, partnership, public limited). It is the common view that project management is applicable in large projects, in bigger organizations. A few studies address applications of project management concepts in retail industry. This case study examines it in retail perspective. There are numerous industries that implicitly or explicitly apply project management principles; the authors have chosen meat retailers to examine the phenomenon. It is a mini case study on a mini entity.

Cheetham meat and poultry (CMP) was established in 2005 to serve the local community with a view to capture lion share of the market. Most of other meat shops were not functioning as an independent concern they work as a part of a cash and carry or a retail outlet. However, CMP deals with meat and poultry products only. CMP is located in the heart of Cheetham village; it has a huge storage facility (cold store) where they can hang 40 lambs at a time. CMP has a 10 feet long display refrigerator and cutting

Exhibit 1	Details of the project				
S. No.	Name	Quantity	Packing size	Delivery date
1	Mutton	300kg	3kg	10.5.2017
2	Chaps	200kg	1kg	"
3	Mince	100kg	1kg	"
4	Chicken	500kg	1kg	"
5	Boneless meat	200kg	2kg	"
6	Drum stick	200kg (800 pieces)	2kg (10 pieces)	"
7	Fish spiced	50kg	2kg	"

8	Fish without spiced	50kg	2	"
9	Chicken mince	200kg	2kg	"
10	Chicken wings	200kg	2kg	"

worktop of the same size, five personnel are working in addition to the owner manager Mr. Shan. CMP owns an electronic cutting machine, a mince machine, lot of knives and another cutlery. Two electronic cash registers are available for customer service. Beef, mutton, fish and whole chicken are principal raw material. The company manufactures 15 products including simple mutton, beef, ribs, mince, and spare parts of animals. Chicken product includes boneless thy, boneless chest, wings legs, whole chicken, baby chicken, spare parts such as hearts and stomach are the key chicken products. (Exhibit 1)

Fish products are relatively limited: whole fish, marinated fish and spiced fish are available. Although financial results are not available yet; the management was satisfied with the performance and perceives it a successful business.

The company has not expended much in the last five years, except hiring of two personnel to meet the increased demand; customer waiting time during peak hours is 15 to 20

minutes; the business customer usually receive their deliveries on time because they place their orders in advance.

The company received an order of 2000 kg of mixed products of mutton, chicken, and fish. Exhibit 1 shows the details of the project/ order for analysis of the case study.

PROJECT PLANNING AT CMP

Purpose of planning, according to Anderson and his colleague are to gain common understanding, obtaining overview of the work to be completed. It lays down the foundation for resource allocation and forming appropriate organization structure for the project that provides guidelines for subsequent work and defining a programme of monitoring and control.

The manager of CMP called a meeting to discuss the project and related issues. The meeting was attended by all the members of the staff since the project was to be completed with daily or normal task (the detail will be discussed later on under the project organization). The manager described the details of the project as mentioned in Exhibit 1. The project will have to be completed within four weeks in addition to the normal workload; the existing members of the team would carry out it without additional hiring or over time arrangements. The manager believes it is viable because all members of the staff are busy only in peak times usually 1100 to 1600 daily. The shop opens at 0900 and closes at 1800 daily, seven days a week; it provides a 4 hour slake time daily for each employee.

Mr. Shah, the manager estimates that CMP would need 30 lambs for mutton products, 1800 chickens and 100 whole fish to deliver the order. The project was managed by five personnel excluding the manager; it took 100 men hours; 1380 packets were made; each item was packed in hard plastic boxes and each packet was delivered to the customer.

CMP will have men 112 hours available within next four weeks, off which 80% of the time will be required for the project.

The manager, Mr. Shah, informed the staff member about time available and the details of work. Mr. Jan said, "we need to make contingency plan for staff members to cope with uncertainties". Mr. Shah replied he had a plan to hire one or two personnel who will work with us as a fulltime member. In this case, we would have 40 more hours available weekly. We can double this by adding another person in our team; all members agreed with the contingency plan and were hopeful for the project to complete on time.

Although all members of the staff were trained to work on any product or able to cope with any raw material, four persons were specialist for dealing with four types of raw material as shown in the Exhibit 2. The purpose of the Exhibit is to ensure that the "right staff" is available at the right place.

Exhibit 2 Specialism of staff members		
Serial No	**Name**	**Animal type**
1	A. Khan	Cows
2	Mr. Bakka	Lambs
3	Arifwala	Chicken
4	Akbar Sindhu	Fish

The next job of the meeting was to allocate the resources. The project uses a range of resources, the worktop, electronic cutting machine, cold store, packing material etc. some of them are shared and others can be used independently; the worktop is big enough to accommodate all personnel at a time. The cutlery is also enough to serve the entire team. However, electronic cutting machine can serve one person at a time. The team members can use it in turn whenever they need it. It saves time without significant loss of productivity. The finished products are stored in a cold store, which has large capacity and is capable to store 8000 kilograms of meat. All the personnel agree to complete the job along with the daily workload. CMP management offers 10% bonus to complete the project for everyone.

As can be seen from the above discussion two teams were formed; one is to cut or manufacture various products and the other to pack them. The first team virtually comprises of all the personnel of organization headed by the manager where he did not do any physical work. The second team consists of four personnel in charge of CMP manager. The details about it will be discussed in the second section of this chapter.

PROJECT ACTIVITY AND MILESTONE PLANNING

Milestones are the key achievements or stages of completion. Anderson and his colleagues view a milestone as "check point in the project, which enables us to ensure that we are on the right track. A milestone is a description of the state the project should be in at certain stages." Milestone should be defined in connection with the solution the project is offering.

Given that, conceptual understanding, CMP defines milestone according to the packing plan described in Exhibit 3 and 4. The largest quantity is chicken-based products followed by mutton and fish. Management has divided the cutting part of the project into three milestones: chicken, mutton and fish, since the former represents 60% of the order followed by mutton 30% and fish 10%. The chicken will be started and finished first; the mutton will be in the middle and fish at the end.

Exhibit 3 depicts the milestones; the length of the bar is according to the percentage of time involved in a milestone. It is noted that there is only one dependency in the milestones; packing needs completion of cutting M1-M3; they had to be completed at one point of time, the M4 can be started than. There is no dependency in the first three milestones, however.

Exhibit 3 The milestones		
	M1 (Chicken)	
Cutting starts	M2 (Mutton)	M4 (Packing)
	M3 (Fish)	

Exhibit 4 Bar chart of milestones

	Period 1	Period 2	Period 3	Period 4
M1 Chicken				
M2 Mutton				
M3 Fish				
M4 Packing				

PROJECT ORGANIZATION

Organization refers to, in management literature, the distribution of responsibilities. In terms of project management the division of activities and tasks. Anderson and his colleagues (1995) believe a project is organized or responsibilities are allocated as full time or part time bases. Team members are relieved from all activities or normal jobs to work on a certain project as a full-time member. Alternatively, they can work on the project as a part-time in addition to their daily routine. It is termed as integration of a project to the existing operations.

CMP management decided to choose the second option because the company has to serve daily customer as a mainstream function. If they chose full time option than they have to hire additional staff for the project or some existing members have to be dedicated for the project. This would put additional pressure on them, which jeopardize the equality of work for which the CMP is famous. Secondly, the managers believe that project is manageable with the existing workload and within the required time framework. Other members of the team were also agreed and happy with the arrangement as it does not disturb their daily routine.

The next question for the CMP manager was to choose mode of organization; theoretically, hierarchical and matrix methods are available. Matrix was selected because its merits outweigh its demerits; it is a better option for decision-making and fixes responsibilities, provides better communication, flexible organization and better use of resource (Anderson et al, 1995). It was important to draw a responsibilities chart to specify key responsibilities for various members of staff which were divided according to the milestones. Exhibit 5-8 demonstrate the responsibilities charts of various staff members individually and collectively.

Exhibit 5 Responsibility chart according to milestones					
Milestones	**Staff 1**	**Staff 2**	**Staff 3**	**Staff 4**	**Staff 5**
M1	√	√	√	√	-
M2	-	√	√	√	-
M3	-	-	-	-	√
M4	√	√	√	√	-

Exhibit 6 describes the responsibilities chart for milestone 1.

Exhibit 6 Responsibility chart of milestones					
Activity	**Staff 1**	**Staff 2**	**Staff 3**	**Staff 4**	**Staff 5**
Whole chicken	√	√	√	√	-

Boneless breast	-	√		-	-
Dram sticks	-	-	√	√	-
Mince	-	-	√	√	-
Chicken wings	√	√	-	-	-

Exhibit 7 describes the responsibilities chart for milestone 2.

Exhibit 7 Responsibilities chart for M2					
Activity	Staff 1	Staff 2	Staff 3	Staff 4	Staff 5
Mutton	√	-	-	-	-
Mince	√	√	-	-	-
Champs	-	-	-	√	-

Exhibit 8 describes the responsibilities chart for milestone 3.

Exhibit 8 Responsibilities chart for M3					
Product	**Staff 1**	**Staff 2**	**Staff 3**	**Staff 4**	**Staff 5**
Fish spiced	-	-	-	-	√
Fish simple	-	-	-	-	√

The last milestone is packing. Exhibit 9 shows the responsibilities of the people involved.

Exhibit 9 Responsibility chart of milestone 4			
Staff	**Mutton**	**Chicken**	**Fish**
1	√		
2		√	√
3	√		
4			√

PROJECT CONTROL

Although the project was a medium size venture, yet some controlling mechanism was essential to ensure the project was on track. The pros and cons of it was decided; each member of staff would fill a progress chart daily showing the amount of work he has done out of the project. This chart has to be checked by the manager daily and instruct the relevant member to catch up the work in case someone is behind the schedule.

Project control "involves analysis the situation, deciding what to do and doing it." It is management of project not merely paper works (Anderson et al, 1995). Control requires reporting of progress and taking correct measure, if necessary. A mechanism should be established to ensure timely reporting of progress at milestone level or periodically. Movement of milestone date, changing objectives, injecting additional resources, and rearranges the workload of team members are typical controlling actions (ibid., p.152). Although controlling activities involve the use of resources, time management, schedule adherence, quality control, responsibility chart, changes/additions, waiting time and any special problems in large projects, yet CMP designed a daily progress report, which usually filled by the team members and examined by the manager to ensure progress at milestone levels. Exhibit 10 reflects a progress report for the first day of the project.

Exhibit 10 The progress report day one			
Team member	Total work load (kg)	Completed (kg)	Balance (kg)
Staff 1	450	50	400
Staff 2	450	100	350
Staff 3	450	50	400
Staff 4	450	50	400
Staff 5	200	20	180
Totals	2000	270	1730

The progress report for day 2 starts with balance of the previous day and generates a new balance at the end of the day. The cutting work was completed in three weeks; the final week was reserved for packing. Eight hundred Kilograms were prepared on the second week and the balance was cut in the third week. The packing was done in the fourth week, while the delivery was due in the same week. The project was completed and delivered on time.

DISCUSSION ABOUT THE CASE STUDY

The project was a medium size venture for the organization however; most of the project management tools and techniques were applied. Important aspect of project was its completion within time that was the major success criteria for it. Other parameters such as budget and quality were not very important because the products of the project were to be use in marriage function. The client needed it on time; the quality was involved in cleaning the meat from fat and other unnecessary elements. All the personnel were supposed to do that for which they were well trained and experienced, so the quality was not an issue. Budget was also not very significant element because the team members were paid as usual; however, a bonus was paid on the successful completion of the project. Since the project was completed on time, the staff was paid the bonus; the project did not overrun budget.

Milestones were identified and defined prudently based on the competencies of the staff; milestones were allocated to all staff members equally but not to the manager because he used to spend a lion share of time in managerial activities.

Consequently, little time remains for operational duties; however, he has done it amicably.

The resources were utilized effectively; the time of each staff member was applied to the best of their capabilities; thus, the project flew in the planned direction over its life cycle. Exhibit 11 and 12 demonstrate the analysis of the project from various perspectives.

Exhibit 11 Product wise analysis of project										
Items		Products								
		Whole chicken	Mince	Boneless breast	Drum sticks	Wings	Simple mutton	Champs	Spiced fish	Simple fish	**Total**
Chicken		500kg	200kg	200kg	200(800 pieces)	100					**1200**

| Mutton | 100 | | | 300 | 200 | | 600 |
| Fish | | | | | | 100 | 100 | 200 |

Note:

The duration of the project was 4 weeks

Each staff has to cut 450kg extra meet except staff 5.

Exhibit 12 Allocation of workload					
Items	Staff 1	Staff 2	Staff 3	Staff 4	Staff 5
Chicken	300	300	300	300	
Mutton	150	150	150	150	
Fish					200
Total workload	450	450	450	450	200

The duration of each activity is based upon the assumption that a member of the staff can cut 25kg of any meat on average. Given that Exhibit 13 shows the total men hours required and total men hours available for the project. Also Exhibit 14 shows the assumptions of various calculations.

Exhibit 13 Activities and their duration		
Activity no	**Activity name**	**Activity duration**
1	Whole chicken	20 men hours
2	Chicken mince	8 men hours
3	Boneless breast	8 men hours
4	Drum sticks	8 men hours
5	Wings	4 men hours
6	Mutton mince	4 men hours
7	Simple mutton	12 men hours
8	Champs	8 men hours
9	Fish simple	4 men hours
10	Fish spiced	4 men hours
11	packing	4 men hours
Total		84 men hours

Exhibit 14 Assumptions of men-hours calculation

Assumptions

1. A staff member can cut 25 kg of any animal in one hour.

2. Total weight of the project 2000kg

3. Men hours required for cutting the project=2000/25=80.

4. Men hours required for packing 20.

5. Total men hours required for the project=100.

6. Available men hours during the life of the project=5 (persons) x 8(daily working hours) x 20(number of working days within which the project is to be completed) =160 men hours i.e. 5x8x20 =800 men hours.

7. Extra time available for daily work=160-100=700 men hours

The above analysis suggests that CMP did more work by applying the principles of project management because daily work was not disturbed and the project was completed as additional work.

REVIEW (CASE) QUESTIONS

1. Do you think project management principals have been appropriately applied to CMP?
2. What other PM Principals could be applied to the case study? Provide an example.
3. Has the project management process including planning, organizing and controlling been implemented adequately? If not, what alternatives were available and could be applied for the efficient use of project resources.
4. The management of CMP opted "integration" strategy. Do you agree with the decision? Why and why not?

5. Discuss the suitability of the case study for the subject. What did you learn out of the case study?

BIBLIOGRAPHY

Aadamsoo Anne-Mai (2010) Web based project management system, MSc thesis, VaasanAmmattikorkeakoulu University of Applied Sciences

Ahmad Ammar et al, (2007). A review of techniques for risk management in projects, Benchmarking: An International Journal, 14(1), 22-36.

Ajmal, M. and Koskinen, K. (2008). Knowledge Transfer in Project-Based Organizations: An Organizational Culture Perspective. Project Management Journal, 39 (1), 7- 15.

Alshawi, Mustafa and Bingunath Ingirige (2003). Web-enabled project management: an emerging paradigm in construction, Automation in Construction, 12, 349-364.

Altar, S. (2002). Information Systems: Delhi: Pearson Education.

Ambler, Scott W. (2008). IT Project Success Rates Survey Results: August 2007, Accessed 12 August, 2014 from http://www.drdobbs.com.

Andersen, E S, Kristoffer V Grude and Tor Haug (1995). Goal Directed Project Management, Kogan Page, London.

Andersen Erling S. and Anne Live Vaagaasar (2009). Project Management Improvement Efforts—Creating Project Management Value by Uniqueness or Mainstream Thinking? Project Management Journal, 40(1), 19–27.

APM (2013). Accessed 12 August, 2014 from http://www.appliedproductmarketing.com/product_feature_vs_benefit.asp

Awad, Elias M. and Hassan M. Ghaziri (2004). Knowledge Management, New Jersy: Pearson Education Inc., Prentice Hall. Accessed 12 August, 2014 from http://turing.une.edu.au/~comp292/Syllabus/KM_Notes.pdf

Azzopardi, Sandro (2010). The Evolution of Project Management, Accessed 12 August, 2014 from http://www.buzzle.com/articles/evolution-project, Accessed 21 June 2010.

Baker, M.J. 2000. Writing a Research Proposal, The Marketing Review, 1(1), 61-75.

Baldrige National Quality Program (2001). National Institute of Standards and Technology, Accessed 2 August, 2012 from http://www.quality.nist.gov/

Baldry, D. (1998). The evaluation of risk management in public sector capital projects, International Journal of Project Management, 16(1), 35-41.

Barchan, M. (1998). Capturing Knowledge for Business Growth, Knowledge Management Review, 4(September-October), 12-15.

Bond, Unyime E. (2015). Project management, leadership, and performance: a quantitative study of the relationship between project managers' leadership styles, years of experience and critical success factors (csfs) to project success, Doctoral Dissertation, Capella University.

Boyatzis, R. E. & Kolb, D. A., (1995). From learning styles to learning skills: the executive skills profile, Journal of Managerial Psychology, 10(5), 3-17.

Brain, M (Canalys), (2010). Android smart phone shipments grow 886% year-on-year in Q2 2010, Accessed 12 August, 2014 from http://www.canalys.com/pr/2010/r2010081.html

Bruce, D.J. and W.B. Martz Jr. (2007). Information Systems Off shoring: Differing Perspectives of the values Statement. Journal of Computer Information Systems. 47(3), 17-23.

Brue, Greg and Robert Launsby (2003). DESIGN FOR SIX SIGMA, McGraw-Hill Publishing Company: New York.

Cadman, K. (2002). English for Academic Possibilities: the research proposal as contested site in postgraduate genre pedagogy, Journal of English for Academic Purposes, 1(2), 85 –104.

Chuang, M., Donegan, J.J., Ganon, M.W and Wei, K., 2011 "Walmart and Carrefour experiences in China: resolving the structural paradox", Cross Cultural Management: An International Journal, 18 (4), pp.443 - 463

Cleland D.I.Ireland, L.R.(2002). Project management, strategic design and implementation, New York: Mcgraw Hill, p. 35.

Canadian Government (2014). Accessed 12 August, 2014   from http://www.gov.mb.ca/housing/coop/pdf/Phase3Fundamentals_Feasibility_Study.pdf

Carter, C. 2004. Harvesting Knowledge from retirees, KM, Review, 7(4), September/October 2004.

Chuang, M., Donegan, J.J., Ganon, M.W and Wei, K., 2011 "Walmart and Carrefour experiences in China: resolving the structural paradox", Cross Cultural Management: An International Journal, 18 (4), 443 – 463.

Collier D A and James R. Evans (2009) QUALITY MANAGEMENT, South-Western: New York.

Collins, C. and K.G. Smith 2006. Knowledge exchange and combination: the role of human resource practices in the performance of High-technology firms, Academy of Management Journal, 49(3), 544-560.

Conforto, E C and D C Amaral, (2010). Evaluating an agile method for planning and controlling innovative projects, Project Management Journal, 41(2), 73–80.

Cooke-Davies et al, Terence J. (2009). Project Management Systems: Moving Project Management from an Operational to a Strategic Discipline, Project Management Journal, 40(1), 110–123.

Corlien, M. V. et al, (2003). Proposal Development and Fieldwork, Designing and conducting health systems research projects: volume 1, The International Development Research Centre (IDRC), Canada.

Crawford, Lynn H and Lynn H (2009). Government and Governance: The Value of Project Management in the Public Sector, Project Management Journal, 40(1), 73–87.

Cusuman, Michael A and KentaroNobeoka (1990). Strategy, Structure, and Performance in Product Development: Observations from the Auto Industry MIT Sloan School of Management, WP#3150-90 BPS.

Debowski, S. (2006). Knowledge Management, John Wiley and Sons Australia, LTD, 17-18.

Deming, W. Edwards (1986). Out of the Crisis (Massachusetts Institute of Technology, Centre for Advanced Engineering Study, Cambridge, MA 02139, USA).

Donahue, K.B. (2001). Knowledge Management beyond Databases, Harvard Management Update, May 2001, 6-7.

Dosoglu-Guner, B., (2008). Organizational culture as a discriminating variable of export activities: Some preliminary findings, International Journal of Commerce and Management, 17 (4),.270 – 283.

Doyle. S. (2005). Outsourcing woes trouble big companies. Internal Auditor. 62(3), 17-19.

Dutke, S. and T. Rermer (2000). Evaluation of two types of help for Application Software. Journal of Computer Assisted Hearing. 16(4), 307-315.

Ebener, S. et al (2006). Knowledge mapping as a technique to support knowledge translation, Bulletin of the World Health Organization, 84(8), 636-648.

Epa (2014). Accessed 12 August from http://www.epa.gov/agstar/documents/conf12/08a_ Ries.pdf

Evaristo , R. and P C van Fenema (1999). A typology of project management: emergence and evolution of new forms, International Journal of Project Management 17(5), 275 – 28.

Ferns, D C (1991). Developments in programme management International Journal of Project Management, 9(3), 148-156.

Fish, K.E. and J. Seydel. (2006). Where IT outsourcing is and where it is going. A study across functions and department size. Journal of Computer Information Systems. 46(3), 96-103.

Francesca, C.M. et al. (2007). Visual Interaction Systems for End-user Development. A Model-based design Methodology. IEEE Transactions on Systems, Man and Cybernetics: part A. 37(6), 1029-46.

Franke, A. (1987). Risk analysis in project management, Project Management, 5(1), 29-34.

Frenzel, C.W. and J.C. Frenzel (2004). Management of Information Technology. Boston: Course Technology.

Friedmann, C. (2004). Knowledge from the workforce, KM Review, 7(4), 2.

Ganssle, Jack. (2008). A million lines of code, Accessed 12 August, 2014 from http://www.embedded.com/design/205604461

Garvin, D., A. (1978). Competing on the Eight Dimensions of Quality. Harvard Business Review, 65, 421-422.

Ghauri, P. et al (1995). Research methods in business studies, London: Prentice Hall.

Gilmour, D. (2003). How to fix knowledge Management, Harvard Business Review, October, 16-17.

Glass, N. (1995). Management Masterclass, London: Nicholas Brealey Publishing.

Golob, K. Majda Bastič; and Igor Pšunder (2013). Influence of Project and Marketing Management on Delays, Penalties, and Project Quality in Slovene Organizations in the Construction Industry, Journal of Management in Engineering, 29, (4), 495-502.

Goraga, M. R. (2008). PAK IT team in Ottawa to enhance trade ties, Business Recorder, 23 April, 5.

Grant, R M (1996). Towards a knowledge-based theory of the firm, Strategic Management Journals, 17, Winter special issue, 109-122.

Greg, H. (2005). Essential elements for managing any successful project, QUE Publishing, Available at: www.Quepublishing.com, Accessed 10 June 2010.

Greg, H. (2008). Absolute Beginner's Guide to Project Management, Rough Cuts, 2nd Edition, QUE Publishing, Available at: www.Quepublishing.com, Accessed 10 June 2010.

Hofstrand, D. & Holf-Clause, M. (2009). What is feasibility study? Accessed 12 August from:

www.exension.iastate.edu/agdm

Hameri, Ari-Pekka (1997). Project management in a long-term and global one-of-a-kind project, International Journal of Project Management 15(3), 151-157.

Hartman, F and Greg Skulmoski (1999). Quest for Team competence, International Journal of Project Management, 5(1), 10 – 15.

Haughty, Duncan 2010. A Brief History of Project Management, available at: http://www.projectsmart.co.uk/brief-history-of-project, Accessed 17 June 2010.

Hoffer, J.A. et al. 1999. Modern Systems Analysis and Design. New York: Addison Wesley Inc.

Hoffer, J.A., J.F. George, and J.S. Valacich. 2005. Modern Systems Analysis and Design, (4th ed.), Upper Saddle River, NJ: Prentice Hall.

Hofstede, G., 2005 "Cultures & Organisations", 2nd edition, New York: McGraw Hill Publications.

House, R S 1988. The clean Side of Project Management, Addison-Wesley, USA.

Hsu, C. and H.C.Wu. 2006. The Evaluation of the Information Systems: A survey of Large Enterprises. International Journal of Management. 23(4), 817-30.

Hydrocarbon Processing, 2002. Hp Innovations, October Issue, 30.

Iqbal, Javed (2007). Learning from a Doctoral Research Project: Structure and Content of a Research Proposal, The Electronic Journal of Business Research Methods, 5(1), 1 - 20, available online at www.ejbrm.com.

Ireland, R et al (2012) Project Management for IT-Related Projects, Swindon: BCS.

ISO (2013). Accessed 12 August from: http://www.iso.org/iso/iso_9000

Jaafari, Ali (2001). Management of risks, uncertainties, and opportunities on projects: time for a fundamental shift, International Journal of Project Management, 19(2), 89–101.

Johns, Thomas G (1995). Managing the behavior of people working in teams Applying the project-management method, International Journal of Project Management, 13(1), 33-38.

Juran, J M, (1989). Juran on Leadership for Quality: An Executive Handbook Free Press, New York, NY.

Juran, Joseph and A. Blanton Godfrey (1999). Juran's Quality Handbook, New York: McGraw Hill.

Kernez H (2017) Project Management: A Systems Approach to Planning, Scheduling, and Controlling, New Jersey John Wiley & Sons.

King, A.W. and A L Ranft (2000). Capturing Knowledge: what managers can learn from the thoracic surgery? Board certification process, Academy of Management proceedings MOC, C1-C5.

Klastorin Ted and Gary Mitchell (2013). Optimal project planning under the threat of a disruptive event, IIE Transactions, 45, 68–80.

Kogon, Kory et. al. (2015) Project Management for the Unofficial Project Manager: A Franklin Covey Title, Dallas, Ingram Publisher Services.

Korda, A.P., and Snoj, B. (2010). Development, Validity and Reliability of Perceived Service Quality in Retail Banking and its Relationship with Perceived Value and Customer Satisfaction. Managing Global Transitions, 8(2), 187-205.

Kotler, P. 2002. Marketing Management, London: Pearson Education.

Kuklan, H (1993). Effective Project Management: an expanded network approach, Journal of Systems Management, 44(3), 12-17.

Kulon, J.P. Broom head, and D.J. Myanors (2006). Applying Knowledge-based engineering to traditional manufacturing design, International Journal of Advanced Manufacturing Technology, 30, 945-951.

Kumar, P.P. (2005). Effective use of Gantt chart for managing large scale projects, Cost Engineering, 47(7), 14-21.

LaBrosse, M. (2008). 10 Ways to inspire your Team, Available at: www.project Smart.co.uk, Accessed 11 October, 2010.

Laudon K C and Laudon J P. (2006). Management Information Systems. New Jersey: Pearson Education, 416.

Longman Dictionary of contemporary English 1995. Essex: Longman, 786.

Mack, R; Y. Ravin and R.J. Byrd, (2001). Knowledge Portals and the emerging digital knowledge workplace, IBM Systems Journal, 40(4), 925-955.

Manthey, A 2006. Capturing Learning: a learning legacy, Leadership, 35(4), 11.

Mariosalexandrou, (2010), Project Manager Job Description, Accessed 12 August from, http://www.mariosalexandrou.com/free-job-descriptions/project-manager.asp

Mathis, Bryan (2014) Prince2 for Beginners: Prince2 self-study for Certification & Project Management, CreateSpace Independent Publishing Platform.

Maylor,H. (2001). Beyond the Gantt chart Project management moving on. European Management, Journal, 19(1), 92–100.

McManus, J (2014). A project management perspective of information system development, Management Services, Spring, 30-36.

McManus, J. & T. Wood-Harper. 2003. Information Systems Project Management. DEHLI: Pearson Education Ltd.

Merchant, K. A. (1985). Control in business organizations, Marshfiled, MA: Pitman

Meredith, J. and S J Mantel (2010). Project Management: A Managerial Approach, Singapore, John Wiley & Sons.

Milunovic, S and J. Filipovic (2013). Methodology for quality management of projects in manufacturing industries, Total Quality Management, 24 (1), 91–107.

MindTools (2013). Accessed 16 August, 2104 from http://www.mindtools.com/pages/article/ctq-trees.htm

Morris, P (2013). Reconstructing Project Management Reprised: A Knowledge Perspective, Project Management Journal, 44(5), 6–23.

Murphy, A and Ann Ledwith, (2007). Project management tools and techniques in high-technology SMEs, Management Research News, 30(2), 153 – 166.

Nagaraj, Srinivasan, M Ramachandra and J Ratna Kumar (2010) Cyclic Approach to Web Based Project Management, International Journal of Computer Applications,8(5), 26-30.

Nicholas, J M (2001). Project Management for Business and technology, principles and practices, New Dehli: Prentice-Hall of India Pvt. Ltd.

Newland Government (2017) Feasibility Study Application Guidelines, Accessed 7 January, 2108 from www.hrc.govt.nz.

Newton Richard (2016) Project Management Step by Step: How to Plan and Manage a Highly Successful Project, Harlow: Pearson Education Limited.

Nikander, I.O. and Eero Eloranta (2001). Project management by early warnings, International Journal of Project Management 19(7), 385-399.

Nissen, M.E; M.N. Kamel and K.G. Sengupta, (2000). A framework for integrating knowledge process and system design, Information Strategy: The Executive's Journal, 16(4), 17-32.

O'brien, J A. 2002. Management Information Systems, Boston: McGraw-Hill Irwin.

Omar, A. (2009). Uncertainty in Project Scheduling— Its Use in PERT/CPM Conventional Techniques, Cost Engineering, 51(7), 30-34.

Orlikowski, W.J. 1993. CASE tools as organizational change: investigating incremental and radical changes in systems development. MIS Quarterly. 17(3), 309-340.

Oz, Effy. 2002. Management Information Systems. Boston: Course Technology, 490.

Pelc, K.I. 2002. Knowledge mapping: the consolidation of the knowledge management Discipline, Knowledge, Technology, and Policy, 15 (3), 36-44.

Perry, J G. (1986). Risk management - an approach for project managers, International Journal of Project Management, 4(4), 211-221.

Portny, Stanley E. (2017) Project Management For Dummies (For Dummies (Lifestyle)), New Jersey: John Wiley & Sons.

Project management institute (2000). A Guide to the Project Management Body of Knowledge (PMBOK Guide).

PROJECT MANAGEMENT INSTITUTE (2004). A guide to the Project Management Body of Knowledge, 3rd ed. Newton Square, PA: Project Management Institute.

PROJECT MANAGEMENT INSTITUTE (2010). Project institution documents, Accessed 12 August from: www.mindtool.com

PulacchiniItaly, Donato (2012). Feasibility studies Methodologies and practices, Turkey Bilateral Cooperation Project.

Raiden, A. B., Dainty, A. R. J. and Neale, R.H. (2004). Current Barriers and Possible Solutions to Effective Project Team Formation and Deployment within a

Large Construction Organization, International Journal of Project Management, 22(4), 309–316.

Rasid, Siti Zaleha Abdul, Wan Khairuzzaman Wan Ismail, Nor Hazlin Mohammad, and Choi Sang Long (2014). Assessing Adoption of Project Management Knowledge Areas and Maturity Level: Case Study of a Public Agency in Malaysia, Journal of Management in Engineering, 30 (2), 264-271.

Reilly, Michael D., Ph. D., Millikin, Norman L., Ph. D. (1996). Starting a Small Business: The Feasibility Analysis. Bozeman, Montana: The College of Business at Montana State University - Bozeman.

Reiss, G. 1995. Project Management Demystified, New York: Taylor & Francis.

Rob, M.A. (2006). Dilemma between the structured and object-oriented approaches to systems analysis and design, Journal of computer information systems, 46 (3), 32-41.

Roberts, G (2005). Groupware as Knowledge Repository, Computers in Libraries, 25 (4), 25-31.

Romney, M.B. and P.J. Stembort. (2003). Accounting Information Systems. DEHLI: Pearson Education LTD.

Rowland-Jones, R (2013). Total Quality Management – TQM, Accessed 10 August, 2014 from www.bsieducation.org/standardsinactipon

Rozenez, S. et al (2004). MPCS: Multidimensional Project Control Systems, International Journal of Project Management, 22(2), 109 – 118.

RUSU, Lucia and Vasile RUSU (2010) Online Project Management for Dynamic e-Collaboration, Informatica Economică, 14(1), 182-190.

Saladis, Frank P. (2003). Taming the Wild Project -- Control Techniques for Project Success, Accessed 12 August, 2014 from http://www.allpm.com/modules.php?op=modload&name=News&file=article&sid=653, Accessed 10 June 2010.

Shang, S. and P.B. Seddon (2002). Assessing and Managing the Benefits of Enterprise Systems: The Business Manager's Perspective. Information System Journal. 12(4), 271-99.

Skibniewski, Miroslaw and Gustavo Vecino (2012). Web-Based Project Management Framework for Dredging Projects, Journal of Management in Engineering, 28(2), 127–139.

Small, C. T and A. P. Sage, (2005/2006). Knowledge Management and Knowledge Sharing, Information Knowledge Systems Management, 5, 153-169.

Smith, M. (2007). Fundamentals of Management, London: The McGraw Hill Companies.

Soderlund, J. (2004). Building Theories of Project management: past research, questions for the future,

International Journal of Project Management, 22(2), 183 – 191.

Srivastava, A and K.M. Bartol (2004). Empowering Leadership in management teams: effects on knowledge sharing, efficiency and performance, Academy of Management Journal, 49 (6), 1239-1251.

Swanson, E.B. and Danes Enrique. (2000). System Life Expectancy and the Maintenance Efforts: Exploring their Equilibrium, MIS Quarterly, 24 (2), 277-97.

The Open University (2016) Project management: the start of the project journey Kindle Edition, www.amazon.co.uk.

Talbert, N. (2002). Getting the most from an Enterprise System. MIT Sloan Management Review. 44 (1), 11.

Teller, J. (2013). Portfolio Risk Management and Its Contribution to Project Portfolio Success: An Investigation of Organization, Process, and Culture, Project Management Journal, 44 (2), 36–51.

The Feasibility Analysis (2013). Accessed 12 August, 2014 from http://msuextension.org/publications/BusinessandCommunities/MT199510HR.pdf

Thomas, J L and Mark Mullaly (2009). Explorations of Value: Perspectives of the Value of Project

Management, Project Management Journal, 40(1), 2–3.

Thomas, J. & Mullaly, M. (2007). Understanding the value of project management: First steps on an international investigation in search of value, Project Management Journal, 38(3), 74–89.

Tudhope, D, P. Beymon-Davies and Mackay, H. (2000). Prototyping Praxis: Constructing Computer Systems and Building Belief, Human- Computer Interaction. 15, 353-83.

UK Association of Project Management (APM), Body of Knowledge (BoK) Revised January 1995 (version 2), Accessed 13 August, 2014 from www.apm.org.uk, Accessed 21 June 2010.

Vail. III, E.F. (1999). Knowledge Mapping: Getting started with knowledge management, Information Systems Management, 16(4), 16-23.

Valacich, J.S., J.M. George, and J.A. Hoffer. (2004). Essentials of Systems Analysis and Design, (2nd edition), Upper Saddle River, NJ: Prentice Hall.

Verweij, Stefan, Erik-hans Klijn, Jurian Edelenbos and Arwin Van Buuren (2013) What makes governance networks work? A fuzzy set qualitative comparative analysis of 14 dutch spatial planning projects, Public Administration 91(4), 1035–1055.

Vordaweb, (2010). Accessed 12 August from www.vordweb.co.uk.

Wadhwa, A and S. Kotha (2006). Knowledge Creation through external returning: evidence from telecommunication equipment manufacturing, Academy of Management Journal, 49 (4), 819-835.

Ward, Stephen C and Chris B Chapman, (1995). Risk-management perspective on the project lifecycle, International Journal of Project Management, 13(3), 145-149.

Ward, V. (1998). Mapping Meta Knowledge, Knowledge Management Review, 4(5), 10-15.

Wellman, J. (2007). Leadership Behaviors in Matrix Environments, Project Management Journal, 38(2), 62-74.

Wetherbe, J.C. (1991). Executive Information Requirements. Getting it right, MIS Quarterly, 15 (1), 51-65.

White, D and J. Fortune (2002). Current Practices in Projects management – en empirical study, International Journal of Project Management, 20(5), 1 – 11.

Williams, B. K. and S.C. Sawyer (2005). Using Information Technology, New York: McGraw Hill Technology Education.

Wilson, J M (2003). Gantt charts: a centenary appreciation, European Journal of Operational research, 149(2), 430-437.

Zhai Li et al, (2009). Understanding the Value of Project Management from a Stakeholder's Perspective: Case Study of Mega-Project Management, Project Management Journal, 40(1), 99–109.

Zwikael, O, Kazuo Shimizu and Shlomo Globerson (2005). Cultural differences in project management capabilities: A field study, International Journal of Project Management, 23(6), 454 – 462.

INDEX

A

B

C

H

I

J

K

L

M

N

O

P

Q

R

S

ABOUT THE AUTHORS

Dr. Javed Iqbal was born on 16 April 1959 in Rawalakot district Poonch Azad Kashmir. He received his early education from Pilot High School Rawalakot and received his matriculation in 1975 and intermediate from Hussain Shaheed Degree College of the same town. He earned BBA with a gold medal and an MBA with a gold medal from Azad Jammu and Kashmir University in 1986. He was appointed as a lecturer in Business Administration in the same university. Later on, he was selected by the government of Pakistan for higher studies and deputed to the United Kingdom. He received MBA from the University of Hull and PhD from the University of Salford. Dr. Iqbal has been working in England in various capacities: professor, director of studies, marketing advisor and academic advisor. Dr. Iqbal returned to Home in 2006 and joined Iqra University Islamabad campus as an associate professor. He became the head of department of technology Management in International Islamic University Islamabad (IIUI). He went back to England for some time and rejoined IIUI in 2012. He joined AKU (AJ&K) as professor and Dean Faculty of Management Sciences in March 2015.

He is a distinguished teacher and world known scholar. His article title "Learning from a Doctoral Research Project: Structure and Content of a Research Proposal" has been classed by one of the professors as the best piece of knowledge for doctoral students of Deakin University in Australia. This paper is widely used and referred all over the world. Dr. Javed Iqbal has been nominated by an international organization for the Award of Distinguished Scientist for his research contribution this year. His books on various subjects are available on www.amazon.com. He poetry is to be published soon as well.

Muhammad Nadeem Khan is in his early thirties; he worked as a researcher with Dr. Iqbal. Consequently, completed his project. He has contributed review of literature for some part of the book.

OTHER BOOKS BY THE AUTHOR (S)

1. Iqbal, Javed Saani (2017) Business Case Studies, available on amazon (Paperback edition)
2. Iqbal, Javed Saani (2017) Virtues of Sickness: Selected Ahadith, available on amazon (Paperback edition)
3. Iqbal, Javed Saani (2017) Prophet Muhammad (ﷺ) as a planning expert, available on amazon (Paperback edition)
4. Iqbal, Javed Saani (2017) Muhammad (ﷺ): His Trials & Tribulations
5. Iqbal, Javed Saani (2017) Sales and Marketing: Selected Ahadith, available on amazon.co.uk. (Paperback edition)
6. Iqbal, Javed Saani (2016) Research Proposals: Contents & Exemplars, available on amazon.co.uk. (Paperback edition)
7. Iqbal, Javed Saani (2016) Responsibilities of Managers: Selected Ahadith, available on amazon.co.uk. (Paperback edition)
8. Iqbal, Javed Saani (2016) Experience: The Journey of My Life, available on amazon.co.uk. (Paperback edition)
9. Iqbal, Javed Saani (2015) Managing Projects, available on amazon.co.uk. (Paperback edition)
10. Iqbal, Javed Saani Understanding Information Systems (2012), Manchester: GRaASS.
11. Digital Divide in South Asia (2011) by Dr. Javed Iqbal, PhD; ISBN: 9789699578120.
12. Managing Risk in Projects (2011) by Dr. Javed

Iqbal, PhD and Muhammad Rafi Khattak; ISBN: 9789699578090.

13. Understanding Project Management (2011) by Dr. Javed Iqbal, PhD and Muhammad Nadeem Khan; ISBN: 978969957845.

14. Information Systems for Managers (2011) by Dr. Javed Iqbal, PhD.

15. Managing strategic change: a real-world case study (2010) by Javed Iqbal, PhD; ISBN: 978-3838330952, available on amazon.co.uk. (Paperback edition)

www.ingramcontent.com/pod-product-compliance
Lightning Source LLC
Chambersburg PA
CBHW032303210326
41520CB00047B/945